Remember me for this, my God,
and do not blot out
what I have so faithfully done
for the house of my God and its services.
(Nehemiah 13:14)

MINISTRY SCHOOL BOOT CAMP

TRAINING
FOR HELPS
MINISTRIES,
APPOINTMENTS,
AND BEYOND

DR. LEE ANN B. MARINO, PH.D., D.MIN., D.D.

MINISTRY SCHOOL BOOT CAMP

TRAINING FOR HELPS MINISTRIES, APPOINTMENTS, AND BEYOND

DR. LEE ANN B. MARINO, PH.D., D.MIN., D.D.

Published by:
Righteous Pen Publications
(*The righteousness of God shall guide my pen*)
www.righteouspenpublications.com

Scripture quotations are from the **Holy Bible, New International Version®, NIV®.** Copyright © 1973, 1978, 1984, 2011 by Biblica, Inc.™ Used by permission of Zondervan. All rights reserved worldwide. The "NIV" and "New International Version" are trademarks registered in the United States Patent and Trademark Office by Biblica, Inc.™

Pictures on cover and throughout in the public domain.

Book classification:
1. Nonfiction > Religion > Christian Church > Leadership

Copyright © 2014, 2017, 2022, 2025 by Lee Ann B. Marino.

ISBN: 1-940197-04-X
13-Digit: 978-1-940197-04-3

Printed in the United States of America.

TABLE OF CONTENTS

———— ★ ★ ★ ————

ACKNOWLEDGEMENTS

———— ★ ★ ★ ————

I N writing this book, I realize I cannot mention every name of all individuals who helped inspire me to write it. I don't remember everyone's names, and I don't personally know every person who has talked to me about ministry, encouraged me in it, and yes, even the ones who have made me step back, stop, and realize just how much change needs to begin to happen in the basics of ministry instruction.

That having been said, I sincerely thank all the individuals who are somehow part of the work of this ministry. My experiences with all of you have inspired me from a deep and abiding perspective to help all of you set up efficient, profound, and well-equipped ministries that will help serve the vision and partake of the anointing found therein. You are all a true inspiration to me and a large part of the reason why, even on my days when I have had enough of the crazy people claiming to be in ministry today, I am able to keep going.

I also, as odd as this might sound, thank every person who ever showed up at an event of mine to try and sabotage it. Thanks to you, I gained many chapters in policy and protocol and have been able to help countless others to handle that same demonic spirit when it rises in someone else. Our ministries now thrive from the ruins as we build from the experiences you have given us. We have learned truth from watching and experiencing rampant errors.

I thank those who come to our events and services, especially as the audiences are starting to grow. I thank every helps minister, appointment, and Ephesians 4:11 minister I have had the opportunity to train, because it is from those trainings I have been able to compile the ideas and chapters for this book. I pray the Lord will continue to bless your work as you bless Him. Thank you all for the encouragement, the talks, the revelation, and, of course, the fellowship.

INTRODUCTION

— ★ ★ ★ —

MAKING MINISTRY WORK

IF one compares the church of today to the church of years past, it appears that many more people are accepting a ministry call than ever have before. The advance of the internet, social networks, and online ordinations makes it easier to claim to be something or called to something without ample evidence to back up an individual's claims. This world of veiled ministry makes it more and more difficult to identify a true minister from a false one. It has also caused vanity among individuals who feel a ministry call exempts them from starting out in helps ministry (and continuing in interest of helps throughout ministry). The result is a loss of helps ministry, service, and a solid understanding of what ministry truly means.

The word "minister" literally means "servant." Whether one serves in the context of the Ephesians 4:11 ministry or in context of an appointment or helps ministry, ministers of all varieties are called to work in service. Certain threads of ministry service are universal, transcending ministry practice, despite one's ministry call or title. Every minister of the Gospel should have ample training in ministry helps, or the work that assists others in the Gospel.

In years past, ministry helps were limited to the work of church service. An individual who operated in a "helps ministry" was one who assisted the leaders at the altar, catching people who fell under the power of the Spirit, providing water to speakers, and hospitality ministry. With the advance of modern technology, the work of helps transcends assistance given at the altar. Helps ministry now includes travel and hotel arrangements, travel planning, ministerial assistance, event planning, relational dynamics with leaders, some instruction, and often substitute or absentee work. Rather than being simple work with a simple plan, helps ministry is perhaps the most complicated, involved, and important aspect of ministry today.

No matter what a minister is called to do, every solid ministry foundation starts out in helps ministry. No effective minister of the Gospel can excel in the work of ministry if they do not understand the basic principle of service underlying all ministry work. Before we can be leaders, we must be good followers. Before being trusted with much, we must be trustworthy with little. All tasks given to a minister in a helps ministry capacity are important stepping stones to larger Kingdom responsibilities. Every great and mighty ministry starts out with the favor of God as one task turns into many, and smaller tasks turn into larger ones.

Through helps ministry, the minister of God learns to be God-centered in their purpose. Ministers who are ordained with haste or without ever learning how to follow effectively are ministers who become a mockery to the office. The minister of God learns to be God-centered as they do things that are of pure and simple service, done without fanfare or applause. Behind-the-scenes work educates ministers in relevance in things others may never see, and how those become powerful building blocks to effective ministry purpose. Contrary to popular thought, ministries do not just "happen." They don't just fall on people because they have received God's anointing to do what they are doing. Ministries do not come about by good wishes, personal hopes and prayers, or even personality or talent. Ministry comes about as ministers partner with God and others who believe in the vision through the hard work of service, dedication, and obedience.

Today's leaders and assistants cannot learn the work of ministry without dedication, discipline, and obedience. Thinking we can do this only when we feel like it, without structure, and without correction will get you nowhere. It proves training is necessary; promotion comes as we are ready to work toward it. What proves you are ready for promotion – is a heart eager to learn, eager to stand obedient, and eager to stand ready for what God has ahead. By learning to assist righteous leadership, we obey God. By learning to do everything required for service, a minister learns the essential heart and purpose of ministerial work. Learning service is a part of growing and developing the necessary outlook and purpose of ministry.

Ministry helps and service also put a minister in touch with the practical side of ministerial commitment. A very small part of ministry work takes place in pulpit work. Ministers of all sorts need to understand the needs of the people they serve and understand how those needs can be met, both practically and spiritually. Helps ministry connects a minister to their audience in a way they cannot get through mere homiletics, pulpit training, and preaching alone. The ability to be a minister who works in diverse areas and is never too good to catch someone who falls or hand a drink of water to a leader is a witness of flexibility, good training, and definitive purpose.

The training presented in this book exists to train lay members, those discerning a call to ministry, and new ministers (first papers or in preparation for such) in areas of helps ministries. It also serves as a "launch pad" to help leaders train both laity and other ministers in the works of all areas of helps. Helps ministries are overseen by the appointment works of bishops, elders, and deacons, and executed by the sub-headings of these appointments, including ministry assistants, armor-bearers, and lay workers. It also extends to those who engage in any form of altar work, church service (such as nursery, children's church, music ministry, audio/visual ministry, clean-up, hospitality, and the like) or service to the people or leaders of a congregation. This serves as the first and most basic training for anyone who believes they have a calling to serve in the Ephesians 4:11 ministry (apostles, prophets, evangelists, pastors, and teachers). Whether you seek to work in helps ministry long-term or believe God is calling you to Ephesians 4:11, this program lays the basic foundations to understanding ministry service and serving God's people, however you are called.

If you're reading this, welcome to the next step in your journey as a soldier in God's army. You're officially in boot camp. Here, you will take the next steps to discovery, service, and purpose. Sometimes it's messy; sometimes it stretches you beyond limits; sometimes it is complicated; but it always brings with it satisfaction as you know you're completing more of your spiritual purpose. Go forth and be all that you can be in God's army!

CHAPTER ONE

---- ⋆ ★ ⋆ ----

PREPARING FOR DEEPER STUDY
AND PARTICIPATION

Do your best to present yourself to God as one approved,
a worker who does not need to be ashamed
and who correctly handles the word of truth.
(2 Timothy 2:15)

OST ministry leaders believe in the necessity of training for those who will be involved in helps ministries, appointments, or preparing for Ephesians 4:11 ministry. This study is different from the instruction a leader may give to the entire congregation of believers on a Sunday morning, or a Bible study class given on a weeknight. When preparing for helps, appointments, or other works of ministry service, it is most necessary, prudent, and essential to train for those positions.

If you're looking to be more involved, you must be prepared for your assignment. This is more than just taking an interest in church, ministry, or the logistics therein. As one in training, your next step is greater discipleship.

Preparing yourself naturally and spiritually

It's great to read the Bible, be a serious Bible student, pay attention to the needs of the leadership in your ministry, and be ready, at a moment's notice, to do things that are needed. And yes, we are going to discuss these very things in this chapter. The reality is, however, that helps ministry is about just that: helping. If we want to help others, we need to make sure we are properly ready to do such ourselves. This means that while helping is great and being available to help is an important part of what you're called to do, you also need to remember the responsibility involved in such.

Perhaps the first – and most important – thing you must realize is that this church or ministry is where you belong. This isn't said in a threatening sense, but you must know that this is where God would have you to be for this season in your life. You are important to its function, to its success, to its growth, and to its purpose. You belong here because God has brought you to this place, and you will thrive here in a special way by participating in the helps development of this ministry. Helps ministry is of no lesser importance than any other aspect of ministry and remembering just how important you are to this work – and how important participating in this work is for you – makes all the difference.

You are important! Every helps participant must take care of themselves, maintain their relationship with God, pursue the essence of spiritual discipleship, and speak up when needs arise (such as taking a break or needing a week off). Helps ministers need to follow good self-care guidelines: getting plenty of rest, eating well, drinking plenty of water, and setting healthy limits and boundaries to allow all participants to engage and work in helps, as they so desire to do so. Don't forget about your relationship with God, either. Be sure to keep up prayer, devotional time, spiritual studies, and personal time with your Creator, as He is the One Who has brought you to this place, in this time, for this work.

Why is training necessary?

Beyond the obvious reasons that leaders do tend to prefer their lay participants and ministers serve the church in a certain way, beginning the work of helps ministries means being a part of the service of the church. It means you are partaking of the anointing present on that ministry in a new and different way. That introduces a new realm of spiritual understanding and growth in your walk with God. You will go from being a recipient of ministry experiences to an active participant in the work of the ministry. This means your perspective on church, on church ministry, on involvement in the Christian life, and yes, even aspects of your walk with God will change. These are not necessarily bad or difficult changes, but they do come with an adjustment. You will meet people you've probably gone to church with for a long time who you never thought twice about meeting and will find some of your long-time friends are no longer where you once thought they were. Your own personal interests and habits may shift. The training you encounter is part of this shift from one way of Christian living to another, one way of viewing the church to another, and one way of viewing service to another.

Getting ready for the assignment

While your leader will most likely begin with specific instructions as to how your position in the church will change, with those position shifts come other adjustments that may not always be so obviously stated. It is important that you immediately begin to make sure you are:

- **Present at all services:** If you are unable to attend service at some point, your leader should be notified. You should also tell them why you aren't able to be there. This is especially true when you are assigned to do something at that service.

  Please know that leaders understand emergencies come up, and sometimes you won't be able to be there. Family problems, medical emergencies, and inclement weather are all situations that arise outside of your control. This is different than not showing up because you don't feel like it or something "more desirable" came along. Being present at church proves it's a priority for you.

- **Attentive during service:** Do not text or surf the internet on your phone during church or Bible study. Don't go to the bathroom a million times to check on who liked your social media status or hear the latest gossip in the line for the bathroom. Take notes on the leader's sermon, follow along with the Bible texts, and make a point to review the lesson later in the week after church is over.

- **Dress for church:** If you are going to be a part of the helps ministries of the church, dress accordingly for ministry. Show up as is in accord with the dress code for that week. If you aren't sure of what it is, do not randomly show up in jeans, T-shirts, and sneakers. Most churches require their helps ministers reflect a good image: suits, dresses, appropriate dress pants, shirts, ties, and appropriate shoes that match one's outfit. See to it that your clothes are neat and clean. Make sure you are properly bathed, and your hair is neat.

- **Watch what current helps ministers do:** Pay special attention to the work, movements, attentiveness, and preparedness of people working in helps ministries around you. Notice how ready they are to do their work and how quick they are to do it. Note their ability to do what they do without disturbing the service. Pay special attention to where they walk, stand, and position themselves as they are needed.

Needed materials

There are many things people tell us we need for study and service today, but many of them are nothing more than a total distraction. For study and service, you need:

- **Bible:** I recognize we live in a digital world, one that uses technology quite differently than when the original text for this book was written. People now can take notes, use a variety of Bible apps, and read on phones and tablets in a way they couldn't in years gone by. While I am not opposed to the use of technology for these means, it is still important you can use an actual bound Bible in book form. Serious students and ministers of God need to be able to use the Bible in bound book form, having the ability to read it without a digital screen and study it for insight and revelation. In some situations, a church leader will require all cell phones to either be turned off or left in the car, and will not permit the use of tablets, especially if individuals are in training. This is due to the temptation to use the phone for things other than just Bible app references or taking notes. The value that can be placed on the use of a book and the ability to use the Bible in book form efficiently and with purpose is immeasurable, especially given there may be circumstances and situations that arise preventing the use of technology in a given time and place.

- **Online Bible resources:** There are many free Bible resources available online. It's beneficial to learn how to use these different online tools. Apps such as Bible Gateway, You Version Bible App, and Blue Letter Bible offer a wealth of Bible translations, reference guides, classic reference books, Bible encyclopedias and dictionaries, and online concordances and lexicons, all at your fingertips. Programs such as Logos, WordSearch Bible, Accordance, and E-Sword also offer similar options for those who desire a computer option in addition to that available on the internet.

- **Bible translations:** Most ministry leaders have a preferred translation. Still, many ministers use various translations in their exegesis and preaching to help point out varying points and expound Biblical text in a greater way. It is vitally important every serious student and minister of the Bible has a translation they can understand in addition to the "old standards" still in use.

Different translations of the Bible exist for different reasons. Some translations serve to provide word-for-word literalism, some try to capture the essence or thought of a passage, some are about capturing general ideas and expound on them in a modern context, and some serve more specific specialized purposes, such as reaching readers who aren't native speakers of a language. While some translations are held in higher regard than others or are considered more "accurate" than some, there is place and purpose for different translations in the work and purpose of a ministry.

I recommend each serious Bible student have the following:

- o King James Version (Authorized Version)
- o Amplified Bible (I prefer the Amplified Bible, Classic edition)
- o New International Version (I prefer the 1984 edition but the 2011 edition is more than sufficient)
- o The Revised Standard Version, New Revised Standard Version, or the New American Standard
- o The New Living Translation
- o A paraphrase (such as The Message Bible or Living Bible)
- o A translation of the Bible in a language other than your native tongue, especially if you are interested in studying or ministering in that language (Spanish, French, etc.)
- o A copy of the Hebrew/Greek manuscript (available in Bible form)

- **Notebook or journal:** As a student, learning will help you gain greater insights into the Scriptures and your relationship with God. As a result, you need to be prepared to take notes from lessons, sermons, and even your own revelations received in the process of thinking about and delving into the Scriptures. Journals and notebooks are inexpensive resources that are great for writing out thoughts and ideas as one goes along. Some prefer to take notes on their phone or tablet. Either should be fine, but it's still good to have a notebook for times when technology fails or is otherwise unavailable.

- **Reference works:** Students have the requirement of research along with study. It's not enough to just have a copy of the Bible and think that will be sufficient for adequate study. Each serious student of the Bible and minister should have the following:

  o Bible Atlas
  o Concordance
  o Bible Dictionary
  o Lexicon (A Bible dictionary focusing on the roots and meanings of Hebrew and Greek words)

Making the church experience transcend into everyday life

The biggest transition for most from attendance to participating in helps ministries is making the leap from faith as a nominal experience to a more intense, everyday opportunity to see their faith through the eyes of service. Where you might have prayed and read the Bible daily (or maybe not even done this on a regular basis), your interest in the Scriptures, in service, and in applying the Scriptures will change – for the better. Do not be surprised if your desire to study becomes greater and you find yourself doing it – just because you want to know God revealed in His revelation to you in a deeper way.

CHAPTER TWO

── ★ ★ ★ ──

YOUR GIFTS AND HELPS MINISTRIES

Now about the gifts of the Spirit, brothers and sisters,
I do not want you to be uninformed.
(1 Corinthians 12:1)

IF you are feeling a pull to work in helps ministries or you are looking to start out in ministry, the first course of action is to know the who, what, where, when, and why of gifts, what are, what they mean, why they are important, and why we have them in the first place. Odds are good that you have, most likely, heard something about spiritual gifts if you've attended church for any period. Do you ever find yourself confused about gifts, especially given what you've heard about them? Has someone spoken a particular gift over you, but you don't know anything about it or what you are supposed to do with it? Do you find contradictory information about spiritual gifts, and wonder the truth about them – but aren't sure where to start in your studies?

If any of the above describes you, you are not alone.

The reason we are discussing gifts is for one simple reason: if you are going to work in helps for any length of time (especially if you hope to eventually move on to more established ministry work) you need to be in touch with your spiritual gifts. You will most likely be asked about them at some point in time and if you are asked about your general direction in helps, it is good to know what they are and how they influence your ministry and work.

What are spiritual gifts?

Let's take the words individually, starting with "gift." We all know a gift is something we are given from an outside source that we do not purchase or buy. "Spiritual" indicates the gifts we speak of are not earthly things. They are outside the realm of this natural world that does not have a natural explanation or cause. You do not operate in spiritual gifts because you trained for them for a long time (and no, this does not mean that ministers are exempt from training – we are defining a word, not bashing all ministry education) or because they are acquired skills or natural abilities. Spiritual gifts are things we have because God has given them to you for purpose and fulfillment within His Kingdom.

Some people seem to display many spiritual gifts; other people have only a few. It is not the number of spiritual gifts that you have, but the application and fruitfulness of them. It is my opinion that most people will operate in many of the different spiritual gifts at some point in time, as they are needed, although this is not necessarily always the case. No matter how many spiritual gifts you have, they are truly valuable and something to treasure.

The cost of having a spiritual gift

If you've ever been given something expensive, you know there is a cost behind it. Precious, expensive gifts must be guarded, cared for, and handled in a certain way. We understand this with things that are expensive in the natural, but we often don't consider it with spiritual things. While many covet spiritual gifts today, they don't understand that having them brings a cost – a value – of great worth. They must be exercised properly and with purpose. Your spiritual gifts must be used for their purpose, and not for anyone or anything else. Any other use is an abuse of them. Nobody gets a pearl necklace and uses it to rig up and tow a car. The same is true with spiritual gifts: using them for a purpose other than what they are for is just as absurd, and just as blasphemous.

What the Bible tells us about spiritual gifts

Many people define any gift or ability they may have as a "spiritual gift." This is a misnomer. It also does not help that the term "spiritual gift" is used in not one, but two different contexts in Scripture, and many do not recognize this when they are scanning over translated Bible texts. To help cut down on confusion, I am going to briefly explain the difference between the two first, and then explain the different spiritual gifts open to the entire Body of Christ.

- **_Didomi_ gifts:** The _didomi_, or leadership gifts, are the Ephesians 4:11 ministry offices of apostle, prophet, evangelist, pastor, and teacher (sometimes called the "five-fold ministry"). We could define these gifts as those specifically for those anointed to lead others in a ministry capacity. They are classified as "gifts" to emphasize leaders are chosen by God for these positions and called to walk in them, rather than being something anybody can do or just anybody does. It proves such works are a gift, not as the result of human effort. These are not gifts open to the entire Body of Christ, but only to those who are in Ephesians 4:11 ministry leadership. The appointments of bishop, elder, and deacon, though important and essential to ministry function, are not included in this list and are not considered gifts.

- **_Charisma_ gifts:** The _charisma_ gifts are spiritual gifts (those we are speaking of in this chapter) that are open to anybody in the Body of Christ, at any time. They are given by the Holy Spirit as endowments for the purpose of edifying the Body. These gifts are found in Romans 12:6-8 and 1 Corinthians 12:4-10 and verse 28, and include word of wisdom, word of knowledge, faith, healing, miracles, prophecy, discernment of spirits, speaking in tongues, interpretation of tongues, ministry (hospitality or service), helps, administration/government, teaching, exhortation, leadership, giving, and mercy. Those who have _didomi_ gifts also have _charisma_ gifts, as _charisma_ gifts are open to anybody in the Body. Not everyone who has a _charisma_ gift has a _didomi_ gift, as _didomi_ gifts are exclusive to leadership.

The Scriptures also give us great insight into spiritual gifts and why we have them. Spiritual gifts, though they are many, connect us back to the one Spirit that unites us, the Holy Spirit. Even though there are many gifts, there is only one Spirit. This contrasts with other religious groups that believe in a pantheon of deities, believing the different deities control certain actions, personalities, and movements. Having one Spirit but many gifts reminds us that God is one, and we, too are all one in Him.

Spiritual gifts are given by grace, for the building up of the Body of Christ, that no purpose and no work may lack therein. Spiritual gifts are given so every believer has a role, part, and work to play in the operation of the church. In contrast to other religions, Christianity is not supposed to be about leadership doing its thing and people coming every week as a non-participatory attendance. Every believer has a role, a part, something to offer in this work of God's love and grace. If you are part of a ministry, do not make the mistake of thinking the ministry is just your "leader's ministry." It should not just be your "leader's vision." If God has called you to be a part of that ministry, that is your ministry, and you are a part of that vision as an active participant. It doesn't matter if your long-term vision is to operate ministry as a leader yourself – you are a part of that work, and you need to see how your gifts and your purposes fit into that vision.

If this is indeed the truth, why does there seem to be a lack of helps in the church today? It seems as if every ministry reports a lack of help, assistance, and volunteers. I wish I could tell you there is only one reason why there is this lack, but the truth is that there are many reasons why there are "lack" in ministry today. Some of them include:

- **Too much emphasis on compensation:** Once upon a time, nobody was compensated for what they did for a ministry, save professional ministers (such as a pastor or leaders), secretaries (if it was a full-time position), and professional services (such as accountants, contractors or other outside sources of professional services). Every other work of the ministry was considered voluntary. People who were part of that ministry were expected to offer their time in service. Offering service made others feel good, as if they were contributing to their faith communities in a practical way. Today, with a church over-emphasis on a misguided sense of prosperity, people expect to be paid for every single action they do, whether they are professionals in their service or not.

- **People think their gifts are about them:** Let's understand something very, very important: spiritual gifts are not about the individual who has them. We do not have spiritual gifts so we can feel good about ourselves, have high self-esteem, or show off in the presence of others. When people think spiritual gifts should be for personal gain or benefit, they will not extend them unto service, because service is not about the individual; it is for the benefit of God's work.

- **Not enough people in a ministry to merit the extensive programs they have:** There are more ministries today – and more people who claim to be called – than there are people to fill organizations. This imbalance exists because people do not understand the difference between gifts and different anointings and do not understand the importance and power of submission to authority. Many ministries were created in rebellion, which has spawned further rebellion, and hampers the growth of valid ministries that exist. If a ministry has under ten people, seven of whom are related to the leader, there is no reason to have 16 ministry administrations within the church. For example: if you have no children under five in the ministry, there is no reason to have a nursery ministry, at least now. Leaders need to make sure they are not creating deficits by spreading the ministry itself too thin and in too many directions that are not necessary for the time being.

- **People are shy about their gifts:** There are those who represent the extreme opposite of what was discussed earlier. Instead of being enamored with their own gifts, people can also be too shy about sharing spiritual gifts or even discussing them. There are those who are so shy about them, you would never even know they have them. If people do not acknowledge their gifts, it is difficult for them to walk in them for effective service.

- **People are not making their gifts fruitful:** Then there are those who know and acknowledge they have gifts, but for whatever reason, aren't developing them. There can be several reasons why this may be the case: fear, intimidation, pursuing the wrong gifts, not having the right grounding and training, and just not wanting to pay the price for those gifts are all possibilities.

- **People are pursuing the wrong gifts:** It's not a secret that the modern church favors certain spiritual gifts over others. For example, you seldom hear about the gifts of discernment or hospitality, but you consistently hear about prophecy and miracles. If spiritual gifts are not studied properly, people can be misled into thinking they should desire popular gifts and not pursue ones that are just as relevant but seldom studied. Suggestion is everything and having someone suggest one gift over another can lead a person to feel the gifts they genuinely have are unimportant or irrelevant – thus, they pursue something else.

The different *charisma* spiritual gifts

- **Word of wisdom:** A word of wisdom is the ability to give insight, relevance, and revelation into a situation that one knows nothing about. It is a form of prophecy but differs in that a word of wisdom almost always requires the obedience and action of the receiver of the *logos* (revelation, essence) or *rhema* (spoken word) revelation. This means a word of wisdom is conditional; its effects and purposes will not be made productive without the acceptance and action of the receiver.

- **Word of knowledge:** A word of knowledge is the ability to give applicable knowledge and advice about a situation that you know nothing about, or a word of insight into something that speaks to the receiver. It too, like a word of wisdom, is a form of prophecy, but differs in that a word of knowledge may or may not require the obedience and action of the receiver. A word of knowledge may just prove God to an individual (making a proclamation about someone's job, circumstance, or age, for example), may call something out (such as an illness, a hidden sin, or a calling that has remained under wraps) or may also offer someone's knowledgeable solutions and advice for a particular situation. Wisdom gives advice and perspective, whereas knowledge gives information.

- **Faith:** We know that, as believers, we are called to have faith. Faith is the substance (or stuff) of things hoped for, the evidence (or proof) of things not seen. Faith is, therefore, a spiritual gift every believer should have. We can imply, however, from the context that there are different levels of faith and different proportions of faith given to each believer. When someone has the gift of faith they have faith as an enduring gift, trust, and focus on God that supersedes

16

everything else in their lives. Individuals with a gift of faith know how to keep the church focused on God, in every season.

- **Healing:** It's easy to assume healing is only about people getting out of wheelchairs or no longer having cancer. The truth of healing is that there are many ways in which we, as people, require healing. To have a gift of healing means an individual operates in the power of God to bring about His needed touch, whether physical, emotional, mental, or spiritual. Most obviously, this is done via the laying on of hands and prayer, but there are those who can bring about healing and comfort through prayer, counseling, and assistance, as well.

- **Miracles:** A miracle is a supernatural occurrence with no explanation in the natural realm. They are things that happen and cannot be explained by science. Miracles vary from supernatural occurrences that relate to magic or the occult because they happen without the different cyclical workings to bring their methods to fruition (witchcraft). Miracles are done by God, and God alone, and serve His incredible purposes. A miracle event would be someone unable to walk from birth suddenly being able to do so due to the spiritual intercession of a minister of God.

- **Prophecy:** Prophecy is a big subject. It is also probably one of the most misunderstood subjects in relation to the believer today. The major reason it's misunderstood? Many assume having a prophetic gift makes one a "prophet." This is incorrect. The gift of prophecy can extend to anyone in the church. God can give someone a prophetic revelation or insight into a situation at any time if they are in the Spirit of God. Rather than being a full-time calling, prophecy moves within an individual with a prophetic gift at God's operation, as needed. There is also more than one way in which a prophetic gift may manifest. Prophecy is not speaking cars, houses, and money over people. It's not telling you the date you'll meet your future spouse or acting as a misguided horoscope at the end of an offering line. True prophecy manifests as an individual moves in an area of seeing or foretelling an event, has a dream or encounter with God that reveals something important about the future, works in writing, music, dance or other arts, or works in prophecy and prophetic interpretation. The prophetic speaks for God, making His will known to humanity. This flows within the prophetic realm, God's presence of eternity (*karios* time), as the individual exercising prophecy conveys His message to His people.

- **Discernment of spirits:** The gift of discerning spirits is an intense experience, knowing what is God from what is not God. Just because something seems to be favorable or un-favorable is not a simple enough explanation to know whether that thing – be it a spirit or spiritual operation – is of God. The spiritual realm is not simple enough to polarize into "like" and "dislike" or the random ways we judge people by what we see or perceive in the flesh. Sometimes God moves in our lives to remove things, and sometimes He moves to give things. Something that can sound great and wonderful can be out of God's will for us, and something that sounds awful can easily be exactly where we need to be for a time. Discernment of spirits is the operation of this sorting it all out – whether something is God or not, and whether or not something should be pursued, entertained, or accepted.

- **Speaking in tongues:** Also called the "baptism of the Holy Spirit" in some groups. We often call this "speaking in tongues," by which an individual speaks in a prayer language of heaven rather than an earthly language. Studies have proven that when speaking in tongues, the believer's language center shuts down and the spiritual center of the brain is active, thus making it a real and viable phenomenon. This is probably one of the most common gifts experienced by believers in the church today. It is also one of the most counterfeited. Tongues is a genuine language, though not one of this earth. Sounds made (such as na, na, na or da, da, da) that mimic earthly tones or words do not classify as tongues. Tongues can serve as a personal prayer language engaging the intercession of the Spirit, or as a word for the entire body of believers.

- **Interpretation of tongues:** If a word is given in tongues for a group of believers, that word must be interpreted. It doesn't make sense for someone to stand up in front of a congregation and prattle on and on in a language people present cannot understand. Interpretation, therefore, is essential, that the word delivered in tongues may be understood by all present.

- **Ministry:** The word "ministry" literally means "service." The gift of ministry is also sometimes called the gift of hospitality or service, because its work can encompass these different things that help people to feel comfortable and encouraged by meeting necessary needs. I think it's interesting that ministry service is noted as being a gift available to all in the church, especially in a time when it is generally believed a ministry to be the responsibility of and belong exclusively to a singular leader. If "ministry" is a charismatic gift, that means people are called to serve within a ministry, whether they are themselves called to full-time ministry work. The Bible does not tell us specifically how to be of service, indicating any gift offered for the work of ministry is appropriate ministry service. Anyone who has a gift to be offered should, therefore, operate a gift of ministry service.

- **Helps:** Helps, also called the ministry of helps and also a part of the works of the church, is the focus of this particular book. Helps is a broad category of church service used to describe all aspects of a church or ministry that relate to the regular operations of an organization. They are called "helps" because they assist the formal ministers of a congregation with areas of church ministry that are too numerous for them to directly run, operate, and function themselves, and because they are a general "help," or service, to the Christian community where they function, as a whole.

- **Administration/government:** The term for "administration" in the Greek literally means "to stand out front." This indicates accountability in action. An administrator has the desire and willingness to step up and lead while implementing the instructions handed down to accomplish this goal. Administration, also called governance, is leadership or the ability to lead, with one major difference. In a gift of administration, one is not just a leader, but also an organizer, an implementer of structure and efficiency. Through a gift of administration, the church can stand strong with details of implementation and order properly answered. Administrators help to continue the structure implemented in every church by an apostle.

- **Teaching:** Like prophecy, the gift of teaching is different from the office of a teacher, with the same major distinction: one who teaches as an office does it constantly and consistently, while one with a gift of teaching does it as the opportunity may arise. A gift of teaching means one can instruct others, and this may come about for any age group or audience, and in many forms (including public instruction, private instruction, media ministry, or writing).

- **Exhortation:** Exhortation is a fancy word that means "to edify" or "build up." In the context of faith, one who exhorts builds up and edifies one's relationship with God and all that goes along with it. It does not merely mean "to encourage," because one can encourage someone into incorrect territory. One who exhorts can break things down into individual steps, make them more understandable, and make the way of God clear in an understandable context. Through God's means to the individual, one who exhorts may speak, pray, counsel, or equip individuals to do exactly what God has for them to do.

- **Leadership:** We've already established not every person in the church is called to serve in Ephesians 4:11 ministry leadership. A further confirmation is the gift of "leadership," or "leading," by which someone is a leader in some capacity, but is not in Ephesians 4:11 ministry leadership. This gift is essential for those in the appointment works of elder, bishop, and deacon, because these roles serve a leadership function. It may also apply to someone who assists in a team effort or work through lay leadership, such as leading a Bible study or home ministry, who is not in the Ephesians 4:11 ministry.

- **Giving (also called mercy):** Much like the gift of faith, there are some endowed with a heart and mind to give. Instead of giving out of mere obligation, giving is a spiritual purpose in

20

their lives. They are eager to contribute to God's work however they can, giving of whatever they have, and are excited to do so. Someone with a gift of giving will budget their money, set aside special time, and make whatever is theirs available for the Kingdom, freely, without having to be consistently asked, without having to twist their arms, and happy to multiply their resources to continue to give for the Kingdom of God. Givers can be found in any capacity in a ministry and will serve as a blessing to both the leader and congregation with their giving.

- **Mercy:** A "mercy gift," as it is often called, is a desire to see an end to suffering. Individuals with this gift are quick to recognize when someone is having a problem or a difficult time, recognizing when something is off or going awry. The gift of mercy sees someone through issues with love and empathy and recognizes the value in those who might be difficult to love. Some Bible translations define the gift of mercy as "giving," because mercy is, indeed, a true gift.

How spiritual gifts relate to your work in helps ministries and appointments

When in a helps ministry or appointment, it's important to know if you are equipped for the tasks at hand. It's easy to take a position because it sounds fun or easy to do, but if you do not have the gifts – the spiritual equipment – to perform that task, it is not going to work out quite like you think, hope, or expect. To avoid disappointment, knowing yourself and your gifts (while remaining open to new revelations about them) is vital. You cannot let anyone just speak anything over your life and chase after every word you think you are receiving about matters – you have to know what God's direction is for you.

It's also important to see how your gifts relate to what you seek to do in ministry helps because the odds are good your leader may assign you to more than one work throughout your helps ministry experience. This is to help you discover and experience different gifts and different ways your gifts can manifest in your life and benefit the church. For this work to be productive, it's important you can express your experiences and gifts to your leader. You most likely have gifts you don't know about, and you may find yourself stronger in different areas than you once thought, or not really called to an area anymore, at all.

Because spiritual gifts are a gift rather than a full-time calling, you may be called to walk in one more heavily than another for a period. The way you discern and learn – as well as gain insight for your walk – is by following God's love and guidance for your life and staying connected to the place where He has placed you (for as long as it may remain).

Understanding different types of anointing

In the original text of this book, I explored the issue of anointing as different from gifts. In the context I spoke of, it is true to say everyone is not anointed for leadership, and gifts are different than being able to handle being a leader. This is true, and I want to clarify the point a little bit further to clarify the difference between the two.

The first thing to understand is that we can have natural abilities, sometimes called talents, and some people will classify such as being "gifted." Natural abilities come through genetics, discipline, and practice, but are not the same as spiritual gifts. In this instance, it's very possible someone might be classified as "gifted" by society, but they are not anointed. While these natural gifts might help point us in the direction of personal interests or things we might like to pursue, they aren't supernatural in nature.

The second thing it's important to understand is that the idea of an anointing doesn't override issues one might have as a person. The anointing doesn't magically transform our personal will, emotions, ideas, or personality. While yes, some things may go along with others, the anointing doesn't change everything about a person. Developing personal character and a spiritual life are essential to everyone, no matter how gifted or anointed someone might be.

When it comes to the Christian life, many people use the term "anointing" to indicate that everyone is called and purposed to do something by God. This isn't incorrect, but sometimes we use the term "anointing" a little too loosely. For one, discerning where you best belong and what you are called to do isn't a singular, one-time process. We will have numerous experiences with God throughout our lives that will press several different situations and circumstances, all of which will challenge our concepts of self (both spiritual and natural). For example, I've spent over two decades in ministry, but the way I minister today is radically different than the way I ministered in the beginning. I've had to step back and think about where God would have me be and assess many smaller situations to best discern how I can serve Him from season to season.

The Greek word for *charisma* does not mean anointing. It is true that it's similar to the word *chrisma* which does refer to anointing, but these two words are not the same. It refers to a special gift or endowment by God, something that God gives us through His grace to build up and empower the church. This means the spiritual gifts given to the entire body of Christ are not given by, nor a reference to the anointing, but are there to serve a spiritual purpose.

In the Bible, "anointing" is an action, not a spiritual gift. For example, church members are encouraged to visit the elders of the church when sick to receive prayer and anointing with oil (James 5:14-16). The purpose behind such an "anointing" ceremony is facilitation of healing. There is also the idea of anointing as a representation of God's grace and unction upon a person's life to do a specific work for Him. It represents being set apart for that specific work within the set apart people as leaders and ensigns of His Kingdom. In the Old Testament, kings, prophets, priests, and items used for sacrificial service were the only beings and things anointed. This relates to being His leader, a worker in His Kingdom, or more specifically within a New Testament understanding, being a part of the Ephesians 4:11 ministry. Referring to this difference, Jesus clarifies for us there is a difference between those who are called (those who answer God's call to fellowship with Him for eternity) and those who are chosen (those anointed for service in the Kingdom).

Thus, contrary to popular belief, not everyone is anointed. There's nothing wrong with this fact. It's possible to be very gifted but not anointed or anointed but not very gifted. It's also possible to be both. Not being anointed for leadership doesn't render someone unimportant or invaluable, but of different service in the Kingdom.

It is the anointing that renders leaders worthy of double honor, because the anointing in which they walk represents God working within them. The anointing represents God is the true operator, leader, and Head of every ministry. Even though God has given us leadership on this earth, leaders are given authority and grace by God to point people unto Him and represent Him in their work. A person's anointing is not their own – it is the work of God within them and their obedience to His call for ministry. Along with that anointing comes a great deal of discipline, service, and yes, difficulty and suffering. It is not something one walks in that makes life easy or glamorous. The anointing simply makes one able to walk out the trials, tribulations, and extensive task of God's ministry.

Just because someone does not carry God's anointing for

leadership does not make them worthless, nor does it make someone unimportant. It simply means that someone does not have the grace of God to be in Ephesians 4:11 ministry. The individual who is not anointed for leadership is gifted and purposed – perhaps even "anointed," in concept, to do or be something else that is just as important and just as needed. God has given every one of us gifts to prove, once and for all, that every single one of us is needed to complete the Body of Christ; we simply have different purposes in so doing.

To be effective in helps ministries, one does not have to be anointed for leadership, but they do need to be respectful of the anointing present in the ministry where they serve. Helps ministries are about walking, assisting, and participating in the anointing present upon a leader and their ministry in a way that can offer a gift perfect for the work or task that needs to be done. Instead of measuring one's self against an anointing, it's important to walk and flow with it, doing and offering what you can in assistance. If you are a part of a ministry right now that is under another's leadership, then you should partake of the offering and grace present there as you work and assist in that ministry, ensuring and assisting its growth and purpose.

CHAPTER THREE

★ ★ ★

WHAT IS A HELPS MINISTRY?

There are different kinds of service, but the same Lord.
(1 Corinthians 12:5)

GOD has established order within the Kingdom of God. Many try to skirt around God's established order in one way or another within their lives (and sometimes, even within their ministries!). There are many who believe that if they have a personal relationship with Jesus Christ, they do not need to submit to higher order. Some believe they do not need to go to church to stay connected to God. Others believe they have the option of adjusting God's order to their concept of order, complete with their own ministry work, titles, and ideas of function.

Within the scope of ministry and modern ideals about independence, all of this may sound fine. Those with these concepts may even have justifications as to why they feel the way they do about these matters. Sometimes they may offer you a Bible verse, opinion or doctrine that seems to support their position. What all these people forget is that God's plan comes with His established order – not theirs. No matter how good the ideas of the rebelliously independent may sound, seem, or be, they are not falling within the parameters of God's established Kingdom order. Even though they may have a relationship with Jesus and may believe in God, they are disconnecting themselves from God's Kingdom.

The Kingdom of God is a part of God's plan for humanity, and most especially, the church. The church body of believers is designed for Kingdom citizenship. Within God's Kingdom, we find God's government, which is essential to His established order. This Kingdom government has a few different divisions, which we will discuss here:

- **The Ephesians 4:11 ministry (Ephesians 4:11-16):** Sometimes called "the five-fold ministry." In Ephesians 4:11, we find the ministry offices of apostle, prophet, evangelist, pastor, and teacher. The Ephesians 4:11 ministry exists as the first and foremost line of church leadership. The offices of the Ephesians 4:11 ministry are God's governing gift to the church: established to build it, defend and protect the church from false doctrine, bring the saints to maturity, equip it for the work of ministry, and establish faith and knowledge of the Son of God (Ephesians 4:11-16). Individuals in these offices are anointed, or set apart and equipped, for the work of the ministry. In this book, we will not be speaking of the Ephesians 4:11 ministry in detail, but I do encourage those of you who are interested to learn more about it to read my book, *Ministry Officer Candidate School* (Righteous Pen Publications, 2026). It is important those working in helps ministries understand the role of each office within the Ephesians 4:11 ministry, especially that of their own leader and the leaders that interact with their leader or as part of the senior leadership in their immediate ministry.

- **The appointments (Acts 6:1-15, Acts 20:17-31, 1 Timothy 3:1-13, 1 Timothy 5:17-18, Titus 1:6-16, James 5:14-15, 1 Peter 5:1-10, 2 Peter 2:19-25, Revelation 5:5-14):** The work of bishops, deacons, and elders (and their subheadings). The appointment ministries are established leadership works to assist the work of apostles and pastors (and, by extension, the other offices of the Ephesians 4:11 ministry) in the edification and building up of the ministry. These works have, over the years, been frequently distorted and turned into offices of the church or the sole works of ministry without understanding their purpose or assistance role to apostles and pastors. We will discuss more about the role of appointments in connection to helps ministry later in this book.

- **The works of the church (Matthew 25:31-46):** The works of the church (also part of helps) are governed by the appointment ministries, but they are done without a formal ministerial title. Churches and ministries have numerous needs that go beyond the formal works of ministry and delve into practical works: directing or singing on the worship team or choir, serving as ushers or greeters, assisting in the nursery or with church school or Sunday school, hospitality ministry, church and yard clean-up, church and building maintenance, decorating for events, church office work and assistance to the ministry, community outreach, and the host of other works that are no less important because they do not have a formal ministry title, ordination, or license.

The three categories above define for us the three basic works of ministry found within the church. These three works keep the church functioning and the Kingdom of God flowing. The second two categories are what this book is about: the work of the appointments and the subheadings of the appointments, which also include the works of the church. It is this work that defines helps ministries: the works created that assist the Ephesians 4:11 ministry in its purpose, so Ephesians 4:11 ministry leaders are able to build up and lead the church. Helps ministry serves as a help, helping hand, and assistance to leadership. In helps, the entire body of believers is blessed by the service that comes forth.

Why are helps ministries important?

The Ephesians 4:11 ministry is a balance of governing authority within the Kingdom of God. Just as in the natural realm, kings and governors operate their realms and nations with assistance, so too God has established His governance and assistance to His Kingdom. It is a perfect system of operation and order.

Helps ministries are important for many, many reasons; there isn't just one. One of the biggest reasons is because ministers within the Ephesians 4:11 ministry need help as they balance governance. It is not possible to do everything needed in a church as a single individual. How do I know this? Because not only have I tried it, so have many other ministers I know. In many ways, we try to be the entire Ephesians 4:11 ministry and the entire counsel of helps ministries, all rolled into one. This has left ministers burnt-out, tired, and unable to complete the work of ministry God has given to them. The Ephesians 4:11 ministry offices work is its own service. It does not exist so God's gift of ministry can be spent doing the work of ten or twelve people. The apostle, prophet, evangelist, pastor, or teacher of God can function in ministry by doing what they do best: offering their leadership gifts to benefit and build up the body.

This also means helps ministry serves an important function for the Ephesians 4:11 minister: they offer help. This is good for a minister in the Ephesians 4:11 ministry for two reasons. The first is that, obviously, ministry requires help. The second is because ministers need to learn to accept help. If an Ephesians 4:11 minister is duly called to ministry, they are duly called for service. They understand the work of ministry exists to serve, and they are so into service, it is easy to forget the need to accept help and rely on others. Even on the way to the crucifixion, Jesus had help from a man named Simon of Cyrene (Matthew 27:32, Mark 15:21, Luke 23:26). The dutiful, purposed church leader needs to learn to receive help and assistance as much as they need to give help and assistance. Helps ministries are the perfect means for such to be learned.

Helps ministries also give participation, as well as a sense of belonging, to church members. It's easy to treat church as a spectator sport. Often people select churches based only on what features or activities they offer, rather than the substance or quality of their spiritual realities. There's nothing wrong with ensuring a ministry can meet the needs that you have (such as nursery or Sunday school if you have children) but attending a church because of what you can gain from being there alone isn't sufficient to produce spiritual development. Ministries do not exist to entertain or fuel personal interests, but to provide places for worship and spiritual growth. Helps reminds us of the importance in being spiritual doers, rather than merely receivers.

Helps ministries are also a great way to allow gifts to come forth. Artists such as Whitney Houston and CeCe Winans began their careers singing in church choirs, for free. They offered their gift – they did not expect to be paid, because they brought their gifts for ministry service. The world is full of famous teachers, speakers, and authors, who just like these two women, discovered their gifts in a church setting wherein they did not get paid. In our modern society, many people expect to be paid to do things people used to just do for free because they were regarded as a service. It is not uncommon to meet people who think singing in church, serving as an usher, playing the keyboard, cleaning the church, or babysitting during service entitles them to serve on the church payroll. Helps ministries resurrect the long-lost art of service: bringing forth a gift or ability for no other reason than the validity of that gift or ability. This gives any gift time to mature, develop, stabilize, and, with God's help, develop into powerful fruit, all in His time.

Helps ministries remind us of the relevance of service in the church. When I first came into Christianity in 1999, the church I attended had an extremely ordered system of helps ministries. Certain ministries were considered essential, while others were considered optional. It was expected that every member of the church was of service in at least one essential ministry. The optional ministry positions were filled by those in training for ministry or who were already working in areas of helps ministries. Nowadays, the work of ministry is viewed differently, because we view helps ministry differently. Regardless of the differences between now and then, helps ministry is about being of service: the call to be hearers of the Word, and not doers only; to wash one another's feet; and to show our love for others by doing for them.

Helps ministry is also, perhaps, the best possible ground for training, both in ministry, and in life. The majority of Ephesians 4:11 ministry ministers started out, somewhere, in a helps ministry. They worked the altar, the nursery, cleaned the church, assisted the leader, helped prepare church dinners, sang in the choir, or taught Sunday school in an effort to participate in ministry. As time went on, they discovered their own ministry call and were better prepared for it, because they knew they'd learned the foundation to great ministry: service. Whether called to ministry or called to participate in church, serving in helps ministries gives a great foundation to knowing the key to success in life is service, not money, power, or fame.

Who needs help?

Helps ministry isn't so much about helping an individual as it is about helping the church accomplish its purposes. Through helps ministries, individuals are helped, but it is not about the individual so much as meeting the needs of all God's people. This means that helps ministries are about benefiting everybody.

During services, special events, and travel, it is obvious that leaders need assistance. They will need help planning, making arrangements, immediate preparations, with altar work, and with the peripherals of the event itself. During services, people will need to be caught if they are slain in the Spirit, helped to their seats when ready to get up, collections will need to be taken, and the church will need to be cleaned. Children will need to be supervised in nursery, children's church, or Sunday school. Beyond service work, those with special needs in the church, such as widows, the elderly, the sick, those with special conditions, caretakers, etc. will also require a special touch of spiritual helps to ensure they are able to remain as members of the community with their difficulties.

If you desire to work in helps ministries, you have a special and important work ahead of you. Know and be assured that God's grace remains with you to complete each task with love and obedience, and that the promise of the prophet's reward (Matthew 10:41) remains with you.

CHAPTER FOUR

— ★ ★ ★ —

HELPS MINISTRIES OPERATIONS

*I know your deeds, your love and faith, your service and perseverance,
and that you are now doing more than you did at first.
(Revelation 2:19)*

THE work of helps ministries does just that: provide help. The work of helps are a part of the essential function in meeting the needs of both leaders and church members, all across the board. For this reason, it's important we expand some of the thoughts found in the last chapter about helps ministries and understand more about the various operations of helps ministry.

Helps ministries do not just happen; they operate. They operate via highly effective, well-structured teams who understand the importance of teamwork and honor leadership and authority. The operations of helps ministries move with strategy and unity, never believing one aspect of helps ministry is more important than another. When we see helps ministry through this perspective, it helps us to better understand the purpose and service involved therein.

Here we are going to examine common helps ministries and what they do. We are also going to look at the different aspects of authority within the helps ministries operations, to better understand how they function.

The appointments

Bishops, deacons, and elders are what are known as appointments. Those who fill these specified positions are appointed for their task at hand, and the specified work does not require formal ordination. They are established for their work via a basic ceremony, celebrated by the local congregation and the apostolic ministry involved. They may or may not be part of ordained ministry, and do not do the works of the Ephesians 4:11 ministry. On the contrary, they exist to assist Ephesians

4:11 leaders. One can be appointed to one of these tasks for a period, or for life. How long one functions in an appointment depends on the project, the individual, the situation, and the relationship between the leader and appointee, as discernment and callings may become a factor at some point in time.

Each of the appointments should be properly trained for their assignment or assignments by the apostle and pastor of the church or ministry and show competency in these works. They should reflect good communication with the leader or leaders they answer to as part of this work and should be able to answer questions, direct and guide, and perform their duties in full accordance with purpose.

If there is a lack of appointments in a setting due to lack of people or proper training, an apostle is able to train and oversee individuals in the necessary work until the time comes when the appropriate individuals are available to assist in the proper way.

Appointments vary from the Ephesians 4:11 ministry in the following ways:

- **They are not a calling:** The Scriptures indicate the appointments are a desired work, rather than a calling (1 Timothy 3:1). This means the appointments are not always a life-long call or anointed work, but rather, a desire to be of service based on the needs present within the church. While they can be life-long or long-term positions (and ideally, I would say they are a long-term commitment), they are not the same as being called – and equipped – for Ephesians 4:11 ministry throughout one's life.

- **They do not represent a formal ordination, nor do they require a formal ordination:** Because the appointments are about helping Ephesians 4:11 ministry leaders, it is expected they work under and in combination with their leaders. Rather than doing a work on their own, appointments are of assistance in accord with a minister's larger work and in line with what is needed. Appointment ministers may or may not be ordained, as depending on the needs of a ministry and the specific work an appointment minister might do. For example, a ministry bishop serving as a regional overseer may need to ordain ministers as part of their work. A deacon assisting in a church's homeless ministry probably wouldn't require such.

- **They do not perform the rites, rituals, and ordinances of the church in the presence of an Ephesians 4:11 ministry minister and never perform ordinations or rites without a valid minister's license entitling them to do so:** Whether to license or ordain one working in appointments relates directly to their duties. The discretion as to what they may or may not do is left to their overseeing Ephesians 4:11 ministry leaders, who are both spiritually and legally ordained for permanent ministry. In the presence of an Ephesians 4:11 minister, the appointment ministries should not perform rites, unless required for some reason. An exception would be a service for a family (such as performing a wedding or baby dedication), or some sort of specific situation requiring a substitutionary minister. They should only perform these duties if they are properly licensed or ordained to do so.

- **They do not operate their own ministries based on the work of appointments:** An appointment ministry is not a ministry for hire. While they may have certain abilities (such as an ability to preach or teach), those gifts are for use with the ministries to which they belong – not so that they can start their own ministries under their titles, working independently as in appointment works.

It is possible for an individual to serve in the Ephesians 4:11 ministry in some capacity and serve in an appointment work in some capacity (for example, the Apostle Peter was an elder at the church in Jerusalem). In my case, I am an ordained apostle who serves as an overseer (bishop) of my church and ministry network. Such is not mandatory, nor is it always the case. In this instance, an individual would serve as an apostle, prophet, evangelist, pastor, or teacher in their own ministry, and as a bishop, elder, or deacon in their leader's larger organization. When one serves in their appointment work, they are not serving as an Ephesians 4:11 minister; their role and purpose is different, and within that position, their work exists to assist their leader, not further their own personal ministry call.

<u>Bishops</u>

The appointment of bishop is one such work that history has twisted, tainted, and turned into something other than its original purpose. The Biblical, apostolic, New Testament bishop is someone who oversees something as appointed by an apostle. Thus, we can understand the appointment of the bishopric to exist in assistance to the ministry of the apostle. In its essence, the role of a bishop is to oversee and maintain a work of ministry directly, ensuring its proper function and regular operation. Bishops are not, within the understanding of the Scriptures, pastors or coverings to leaders, as the term is commonly (and incorrectly) used today. While they may serve as overseers of a congregation, it is under the oversight of an apostle, and for the purpose of ministry communication, function, and spiritual preparation.

In the context of helps ministries, a bishop oversees an aspect of church ministry that helps the leaders to function. It may be in a more official capacity, such as overseeing the basics of a congregation or a region, and serving as a liaison to the apostle, or it may be more in a helps capacity, such as overseeing the finances of an organization or a group of ministries. In the most common association, bishops often attend to the spiritual needs of a region or group of ministries, assisting apostles in function.

Elders

The appointment of elder is a little different than many use it today. Elders are not pastors, but rather individuals appointed in each congregation by an apostle for the regular function and assistance of the ministry. Where bishops exist to assist apostles, elders exist to assist pastors. Extensive discourse is given to the works of elders in the New Testament (Acts 20:17-31, 1 Timothy 5:17-18, James 5:14-15, Revelation 5:5-14). From what we can see in the Scriptures, the work of an elder relates to government, instruction, and meeting the needs of the congregation members on a regular basis. Their work is specific to the spiritual needs of the congregation, rather than general function in social ministry.

There are many ways elders can assist in church function. These different ways include everything from assisting in the teaching needs of a ministry to private counsel, hospital and home visits, overseeing specific local ministries (such as women's or men's ministry) or any other function a church may need. Unlike bishops, elders assist exclusively in their local congregations.

Deacons

The appointment of deacons serves one purpose: service. Whether assisting leadership or assisting the congregation through social work (Acts 6:1-15, 1 Timothy 3:8-13), the role of a deacon is not what most denominations have concocted. Deacons do not run the church from the pew, nor do they have the power to outvote a pastor, control the money or church finances, or decide who or who should not be in leadership.

Simply put, deacons exist to do social and practical work, meeting practical needs that exist among leaders and congregations. Rather than being an office of overseeing, deacons are the doers of the church. Deacons are about service, wherever it is needed. The work of an "armor bearer," or "leader's assistant," for example, can fall into the work of the diaconate. Those who help to operate practical ministries of service, such as widow's care or shut-in ministries, are also doing the work of the diaconate.

Leadership assistance (armor bearers, assistants, adjutants, etc.)

I do not advise everybody who desires this ministry be arbitrarily assigned to fill it. The armor bearer is a special title for a spiritual assistant to a ministry leader. It's identity comes from the Old Testament armor bearers who assisted governmental leaders in battle. Whether or not the role is appropriate for New Testament leaders is of some debate. However, whether a leader's assistant is called armor bearer, assistant, adjutant, or something else, the idea that leaders need help isn't an unbiblical idea.

Different leaders have different needs when it comes to ministry assistance. Some require assistance that's more practical (such as help with housekeeping or organization), and others require more spiritual assistance. (I'm of the opinion that ministry leaders should not expect their assistants to do things like housekeeping, but that's just my perspective). Assistants also often are involved in regular church events, preaching, travel, and other ministry activities.

First and foremost, assistants should be available for spiritual needs: to pray, spiritually empower, and support, as possible. This work involves extensive spiritual discernment, intercession, planning (including assisting visiting ministries and making their hotel and airline arrangements), virtual ministry (assisting in the work of ministry online and the virtual image of the ministry), and practical time, as the individual in this role assists the minister of God in their God-ordained purpose. Those who serve in direct leadership assistance should be fully trained in appointments and the work of ministry, and should show forth good character, spiritual maturity, and understand their purpose.

Overseeing

Bishops are appointed to oversee various ministry work as assigned by an apostle covering the leader and work of a congregation. A bishop may oversee more than one ministry work, a specific ministry work, or a specific aspect of the ministry. The specification of just what a bishop "oversees" is decided according to the needs of an organization and may vary. Whatever it is, the bishop's work is called to reflect efficient governing and good stewardship.

As discussed earlier, bishops are typically associated with assisting in spiritual needs. Bishops might help establish congregations, fill in when there's a pastoral vacancy, help train ministers-in-training, assist in ordinations, or help mediate issues between members and leaders. Bishops might also oversee specific aspects of larger ministries, such as regions, special interest ministry groups, finances, or administration.

Ministerial function, assistance, and teaching

Elders are responsible for assisting pastors and other church leaders in the teaching, function, needs, and executing spiritual purpose within the local church. Elders ensure the needs of people are met, primarily spiritual needs: receiving prayer, altar work functions and flows freely, teaching is available throughout the necessary ministry avenues, individual instruction or counsel as needed, and situations which involve legalities and governance are handled in cooperation with the Ephesians 4:11 ministry offices.

Social work

We will discuss more about social ministries later in this chapter. In summary, any ministry that relates to people, especially the needs of people, falls into the category of social ministry. As deacons are the social workers and doers in the church, it is their responsibility to govern those who desire to assist in these works as volunteers.

The work of the diaconate is vital to ensure church can function spiritually, because social needs are met. It's difficult to focus on spiritual things when natural cares weigh on one's mind. Things such as hunger, thirst, lack of clothing, and an inability to survive within society all weigh on the minds of those who are often the most vulnerable. Social needs prove God cares about every part of us as well as the need for humans to interact, as they are interconnected within society.

Volunteers

Individuals who participate in helps ministries without formal appointment are church volunteers. These people are members of the congregation or members of another congregation or community who come forward to offer the gifts they have. Volunteers offer their time and skills and are, therefore, not compensated for their service. The volunteers of a project are supervised by an appointment ministry, depending on what the work is. For example, if a member of the church volunteers to help with the shut-in ministry, they would be supervised by a deacon. Those who assist in the altar ministry would be supervised by an elder, and those who assist in the organization of helps ministries would be supervised by a bishop.

People who assist and volunteer in ministry should not be turned away because they are not ordained, nor do they fall under the heading of an appointment. On the contrary, everyone who is interested in service within the church should be allowed to step up and participate as they so desire, if they are able to follow the guidelines and participate within the bounds of decency and order.

The works of the church

As we discussed in the last chapter, the works of the church (helps) are governed by appointments leader, but are run by volunteers, the work of which we just defined. These specific ministries, though governed by appointment ministers, largely function due to volunteer laity who care about the future of the church and want to be of service, as is defined by their faith.

The members of each church or ministry should be encouraged to participate in at least one ministry of the church open to volunteer/member participation. Rather than emphasizing only the Ephesians 4:11 ministry and appointments as ministerial service, let congregation and ministry members know how important it is to be active and participating in church service. Service in church does not begin, nor end at the altar; it begins with every member remembering Jesus' call to serve even the least of these, because when we do so, we do it unto Him (Matthew 25:40,45). Church and ministry participation do not begin, nor end, with weekly service attendance and tithes and offerings, although these things are important. Attending and being part of a church or ministry body is about being a part of the Lord's Body, and everyone learning to do and function within their unique call and purpose for the benefit of God's Kingdom (Luke 19:11-27, Ephesians 4:1, 2 Peter 1:10). We learn how to do this better in our own lives and communities as we learn first how to do it within churches and ministries.

Each church and ministry operate their own specific works, based on the needs present within that organization. Congregation members and participants should be aware of the different opportunities they have to participate in these ministries and should be appraised for their needs and vacancies therein. Members should also understand the importance of volunteer participation for church functions, conferences, special services, and other events that are outside the normal weekly schedule for the congregation.

Those who participate as volunteers in the works ministries should be required to go through training or rehearsals, depending on the nature of the work. They should also be required to meet back from time to time, both updating and celebrating the volunteers for their work. Church volunteers, who are taking time out of their very busy lives to be of service to the church, should know they are appreciated and loved by all in their community.

Any of these specific groupings of church work can be combined as is necessary. There may also be other works unique to a community that are not mentioned here or some listed here that may be eliminated due to the needs which may exist in that specific church or ministry. The works listed below are listed to give a general idea of function and purpose as well as see how each aspect of church ministry working with the others brings about a solid church foundation for success.

Announcements

Someone might question the announcements as a ministry, but the truth is this: if essential information is not conveyed to the congregation, essential issues are never resolved. The announcements should ideally be handled by two people per necessity. For example: if a church has multiple services in a weekend and the people who attend each service are different (meaning the people who make the announcements won't be at each service), two people should be selected for each service as necessary. Having two people gives the opportunity for teamwork, a rotational schedule, and a substitution as is necessary.

An announcement schedule should be made aware for everyone in the church (both leaders and members) so all announcements may be properly organized for presentations on services. For example, for a message to be conveyed via announcements for a Sunday service, it must be received by the announcements ministry no later than Friday at 5 PM. Those who are in this work should consult with leaders for necessary announcements each week. Topics to be included in announcements include happenings among the congregation (individual in the hospital, needs prayer, etc.), church or ministry events, volunteers needed for a specific ministry, upcoming meetings, community church events, classes, things that pertain to order or function within the church or ministry, and anything else deemed necessary or essential to the church. At the end of the announcements, it should be asked if there are any additional announcements to add.

Those who make the announcements should dress appropriately in church attire as determined by the church or ministry leadership. They should carry themselves appropriately, show up on time, and behave with decency and order.

Office/business work

The office work of the church or ministry pertains to many very serious business aspects of ministry that must be kept at a close watch and with proper organization. Failure to keep proper records can result in trouble with the IRS, state governments, or loss of property and assets all together. On a smaller level, problems with office staff can cause a church to fail, shrink, or simply not grow like it should.

Office work requires efficiency based on the size of a ministry or congregation and the unique needs it has. Some ministries have the option to outsource some business needs to an agency, such as a CPA or accountant. Others do everything in-house, relying on church volunteers. Those who assist with office duties should be competent, trustworthy individuals who are well-equipped for the job. All should be well-versed in computer skills, know how to use basic software required for ministry operation, basic layout for bulletins and booklets, understand filing systems, able to answer the phone, book appointments, assist with scheduling, non-profit tax reporting, and other essential duties as determined necessary by the ministry.

Altar work

Altar work is a loaded term to many ministries because it encompasses a wide expanse of areas. The basic definition of altar work is every attentive work that attends to the needs present at the altar, both within ministers and members or guests. Altar work begins prior to service, it ends after each service and requires extensive training to ensure proper flow.

Altar work includes the following areas:

- Providing water/beverages to ministers
- Making sure the altar area is clear and ready for service with essential items the leader and/or minister will need
- Removing shoes or other items from the path of a minister or preacher
- Praying for and monitoring someone who starts to shout or fall out, to ensure they don't drip or fall on the floor
- Assisting at times of prayer and laying on of hands by holding anointing oil, catching people who fall, covering people who fall, and assisting people to return to their seats
- Helping to keep order during altar calls
- Make sure items for the altar are put away, cleaned, and ordered after service
- Working in combination with ushers and greeters to decorate the church for special events

Ushers/greeters

Ushers and greeters have the basic function of greeting people when they come in church, helping them to their seats, and dealing with general congregational needs as arise during services. While altar workers are busy attending to the work of the altar, ushers are busy attending the work of the congregation during services and events. They should be available as often as the church or ministry is available for public service events that involve greeting, seating, and order. They are required to dress in church attire or attire as specified by the church or ministry, and follow the instructional orders as given. Ushers and greeters need extensive training and supervision to ensure the job is done properly and rightly.

Ushers and greeters work in the following areas:

- Greeting and seating people before and during services
- Guiding traffic in the parking lot
- Assisting the handicapped during services
- Handing out church bulletins
- Give directions (bathrooms, classrooms, etc.)
- Taking and counting the collection
- Preparing communion elements, distributing them after consecration, and then cleaning up after communion
- Making sure sanctuary is prepared before service and kept neat after service
- Working in combination with altar workers to decorate the church for special events

Praise and worship team/choir

Historically speaking, churches were often noted for their quality by the quality of their choirs. Choirs were people's first impression of a church, and for good reason: a good choir gives the display of a unified church. The ability to harmonize, blend, and sing with great power takes incredible unity, especially given many church choirs function only one or two rehearsals per week, at most. Choirs often have many members, with a director, who may or may not play an instrument while they lead the group.

Choirs are typically accompanied by an organ or piano and divided up by choral arrangement into two parts, four parts, or eight parts. Some choirs require an audition to sing, others allow anyone to participate who desires to do so. Many have solo options and select soloists based on try-outs or histories of musical selections. In some churches, cantors, or individuals who sing solo parts and lead the choir via song, are used, but these are typically found in only high Protestant or Catholic churches.

In more modern times, praise and worship teams have replaced choirs in many churches, or choirs are used as back-ups to praise and worship teams. Praise and worship teams may be accompanied by CD backing tracks, keyboards, organ or piano, percussion instruments, or sometimes, full bands. Praise and worship teams often have fewer members than choirs and may have more requirements to participate. A participant may be required to attend frequent rehearsals, write their own music, play an instrument as well as sing, and sing in a certain range or have a certain sound.

Some churches have praise teams, some have choirs, and some churches have both. Many churches strive to incorporate both traditional and modern arrangements in their styles. Both choirs and praise and worship teams have the requirement to attend rehearsals, follow good instructional directions, dress according to code, be available for various events of the ministry, and sometimes, even be available to attend services, events, and competitions in various areas.

Audio/visual ministry

Audio/visual ministry is one of the most overlooked, and yet essential aspects of modern church ministry. In modern churches and ministries, audio/visual work provides sound, equipment, and visual cues for both leaders and attendees. The audio/visual ministry may be something done by a professional in that field, or someone who just finds it an interesting hobby. Most audio/visual ministry technicians spend many hours perfecting things, and it is required that one be computer literate to work in this area.

Audio/visual workers work in the following areas:

- Run sound booth/sound equipment
- Setup microphones
- Set up and operate visual screens
- Using software, prepare visual cues for words for songs
- Record (audio, video) of services
- Duplicate CDs/DVDs
- Edit audio/visual files for television, radio, duplication, and internet distribution
- Website design/internet ministry
- Recommend software/programs for use in audio/visual ministry
- Monitoring live streaming and church short videos or advertisements
- Handling required distribution and licensing

Arts/dance ministry

Arts ministries are one of the fastest-growing aspects of church ministry today. In this category, we consider all areas of arts that are non-musically related, including dance, mime, theater/drama, movement, poetry, readings, or other arts-related activities that can be done as part of worship services or part of ministry in general. Volunteers for arts ministries should be advised of rehearsals, costumes, necessary time and travel, and required availabilities for services, special events, and beyond.

Children's ministry (Children's church, nursery, Sunday School, Vacation Bible School)

Special-interest ministries are a challenge to govern without the guidance of a leader who often helps to shape the vision. I am mentioning children's ministry first because it is often a special-interest ministry that demands the most time, attention, and continual involvement from the congregation. Children's ministry encompasses nursery, children's church and/or Sunday school, and special meetings or events, specifically for the children of the church.

Children's ministry requires extensive planning. Classes, events, and services that pertain to children must be properly stocked, timed, and staffed. Educational materials and activities should be age-appropriate, suited for the group present, and suited for the size of the group. This means church volunteers are especially important, because children do not have self-governing powers and require extensive teaching and supervision. As a result, children's ministry activities need to be divided up by age groups and size of groups.

A volunteer for children's ministry should be extensively trained and show an aptitude for working with children. As we are dealing with children in this ministry, volunteers should have clean legal records as applies to interaction with minors and should not be given to drugs, alcohol, abusiveness, or other unseemly behaviors. Volunteers should also be carefully guided in appropriate measures for discipline and age-appropriate ways to handle various issues.

Children's ministry volunteers should be apprised of the needs that will call them to duty beyond service times and days, and informed that, in the case of children's church or nursery, will draw them away from regular weekly service. For this reason, rotational schedules should be used, to give everyone a chance to visit regular service. As a thanks to those who miss service to engage in childcare or education, a recording of the message should be provided to them, at no cost.

Youth ministry

Youth ministry is often the most difficult ministry to generate volunteer participation. The reason why it is so difficult to garner participation is simple: teenagers have a bad reputation. This reputation is fostered through years of failing to meet the needs of teenagers through church ministry. Other organizations, such as Boy and Girl Scouts, have long histories of teenage participation, interest, and involvement, despite the age group.

Teens are not children, nor are they yet adults. They often require supervision, but not nearly as much supervision as is required for very young children. At the same time, youth ministry still demands time, attention, and congregation involvement.

Youth ministry is typically for kids who are older than children's ministry, but not old enough for adult ministries. Most youth ministries start around seventh grade and go through the senior year in high school (about ages twelve to eighteen). Youth ministry encompasses youth groups, youth-oriented conferences and events, Sunday school for youth, and special meetings, trips, or events, specifically for the youth of the church.

Like children's ministry, youth ministry requires extensive planning, but for different reasons. The events and classes for a youth ministry need to both reach out to and address the specific issues, needs, and problems teens face today, with comprehensive and powerful solutions. Unlike children's ministry, youth are of the age to where they can participate in the process. Youth participants should offer and foster discussions on topics and things they'd both like to learn and study in the Scriptures. They should also give feedback on projects they'd like to do and ministries they would like to participate in.

Youth ministries should work both divided up into age groups and work together as one large group for events, projects, and service activities. The age-group divisions relate to teachings and concepts, while the work as one large group helps them to learn to relate to church with people of different ages and stages of learning.

Youth should be a part of the general worship service of the church and should have various ways in which they participate in the services. They should also be active participants in the various ministries of the church. Each youth in the church should select at least one helps ministry of the church to participate in per year. They should also be taught about giving, tithing, and participating in events, such as conferences and Bible studies.

When a youth shows interest in ministry, they should be offered a mentoring with a church leader. Youth who are interested in ministry should be educated in such and given the opportunity to begin peer mentorship/leadership training. This special-interest program within youth ministry gives interested youth the opportunity to gain basic leadership skills that will help them to work as peer leaders among their own age group and develop important techniques to help with both life and ministry.

Youth ministry should also participate in community service. It should be a goal of each youth ministry to complete so many hours of community service per year. Community service should not be random, but should seek to expand the world of youth, causing them to see the problems and challenges others face. Community service should give them a sense of pride and hope, knowing that while problems exist in the world, there are things they can do to help make the lives of others better.

Youth ministry shouldn't be all study and service but should also include social activities and gatherings. Churches all too often forget to offer youth events that help them get to know others who are their own age within their church congregation. When available, youth events should include youth of other churches as well, so those involved in a youth ministry can see that being a Christian doesn't mean being socially inept, boring, or bland.

Youth ministry requires planning. Even though teenagers are not children, they do require some supervision. Educational materials, films, and work should be screened for content. Inappropriate content and language should be monitored. Volunteers for youth ministry should be trained and show interest and aptitude for working with teenagers. Since we are still dealing with minors, volunteers should have clean legal records as applies to interaction with minors and should not be given to drugs, alcohol, abusiveness, or other unseemly behaviors. Volunteers should also be carefully guided in appropriate measures for discipline and age-appropriate ways to handle various issues.

Youth ministry volunteers should be apprised of the needs that will call them to duty beyond service times and days, prepared for trips that may take them away overnight, and the requirements to participate, along with the youth, in service and church activities.

Special interest ministries

Not every ministry feels the need to have a men's or women's ministry, especially if the ministry doesn't desire to fall into specified gender binary categories. As a result, I have changed this section to "special interest ministries," because such can encompass any ministry work that targets a specific ministry group (outside of children and youth ministries). Thus, "special interest ministries" can cover men's or women's ministry, singles or married ministry, ministry groups that reach out to young adults, LGBTQ+ individuals, seniors, or any other group that might be representative of a ministry body and in need of special interest or counsel.

The good news about adult ministries is that they do not require the same level of supervision that children's and youth ministries require. As adults are old enough to self-govern, they do not require constant or moderate supervision. Most adult ministries simply need the necessary guidance and teaching to function as a ministry and understand the guidelines of participation.

Special interest ministries are typically for adults twenty-one and older or may include older teens (sixteen and up) sometimes, as well. These ministries are typically set apart by a common need or interest and are open to anyone who may be representative of this community, or interested in learning more about it. The basic premise of such a group is to host activities, education, spiritual empowerment, and revelation specifically needed for these individuals. The goal is to create bonds, show those of these groups that they do have a place within the church, and to offer God's insights in a manner that are relatable and relevant to those who participate.

It is very important that all staff have the necessary education and training to work with such specified groups. The minister of these ministries should be available for counseling to those who participate in it, thus having training in their area of ministry. It's also important to avoid treating adults like children. Be sure to receive feedback, suggestions, and participation from the ministry participants on what is needed and what should be done.

Even though special interest ministries don't require the same level of governance as children's ministries, they do require planning. Meetings, conferences, socials, and events should be well-planned and well-thought out. Educational and spiritual works should address specific issues, needs, and problems faced by men and women today, with comprehensive and powerful solutions.

A side note: participants in special interest ministries should be a part of the church as a whole and should be involved in worship services, church ministries as volunteers, and active in giving and tithing. These special-interest ministries are also a great opportunity to invite and incorporate visitors from other churches and community members, as well. Also, never forget about the option of community or church service, such as work in the community, decorating or cleaning the church building, or other productive work that can be done as part of a special interest gathering.

Volunteers for special interest ministry should be trained for their work, trained in whatever aspect of the ministry they will need to assist in, and be prepared for the varied work that goes along with the ministry, including travel, retreats, and occasional overnight trips.

Building maintenance and hospitality

I have put these two works together because they go together, even though we don't often consider that they go together. If a building is not well cared for, it is not a seat for hospitality. To have a functioning place to be hospitable, ministries need to maintain their buildings as well as provide comfort and refreshment to their leaders, guests, and congregation members.

Building maintenance is one of the most difficult areas to enlist volunteers. It's not a showy point of service and requires a lot of hard work. Making the commitment to participate in building maintenance is ongoing, weekly, and time consuming. It is also, in many ways, a foundational aspect to the continuation of the ministry. Good building maintenance avoids lengthy lawsuits, insurance problems, and other issues that can relate to expense and time in the long-term.

Building maintenance includes:

- Monitoring and calling in repairs, as necessary
- Maintaining the parking lot area, keeping it clean and free of debris
- Taking care of the lawn work and maintenance or hiring a suitable party to do so
- Keeping the sanctuary, hallways, classrooms, bathrooms, and main areas clean
- Making sure the church or ministry has the appropriate tools to perform necessary maintenance

Hospitality ministry is often thought of as the "food ministry." In some ways this is accurate, but in others, it doesn't go far enough. Hospitality is about ensuring the comfort and welcome of leadership, members, guests, and visitors to a place. It is a spirit of welcoming rather than just about food service, although hospitality does include that, as well.

Hospitality ministry includes:

- Providing a welcome committee for special events at the church or ministry
- Being a go-to when water or other items are needed during a service
- Planning social gatherings and after-service or conference social events
- Food and beverage preparation for such events (including utensils)
- Decoration for such events
- Clean-up after events

Social outreach ministries (homeless, widows, clothing drives, street evangelism, food banks, shelter ministries, prison ministry, drug/alcohol ministry, community counseling projects, involvement with community projects, etc.)

I have grouped social outreach ministries together because most churches do not take on more of these ministries than they can practically handle. Social outreaches are works that relate to people and the meeting of their practical needs. These include the works listed above, but do not exclude other works of a church, which may include day care, job skills, literacy, GED preparation, or a host of other outreaches geared to assist and empower the community.

Social outreaches are essential and important because they encourage the church and its members to be active participants in the world they live. Being a Christian does not mean running from or hiding from the various issues our world faces. Jesus calls us to be His hands and feet in this world, helping where we can, doing as we would do unto Him.

Volunteers for these ministries need training and preparation. All involved should be apprised of the requirements in time and qualifications to participate. Anyone is welcome to participate in them, and community involvement is also welcome for donations and assistance.

Street evangelism/witnessing

Do you desire to get out there and see that others learn about the Lord? Street witnessing is a great ministry to participate.

As street witnessing is done in public, those who participate should be infored of requirements in attire (this is a dress down occasion, not a dress up time), the dangers involved in where they may be going (dangerous areas, college campuses, gang locations, etc.), and trained in how to start conversations with people and distribute information. All should be informed as to the time requirements and the purpose in doing this work. Young children should not be included, for their own safety and the ministry's liability.

The church or ministry you are a part of may have all these outreaches, only some of them, or may have additional ones that are not listed here. They may do some of them differently, due to the needs present in your situation. All of the information presented here gives guidelines as to how these ministries can function best efficiently. The tips and structure put into place can apply to any type of ministry outreach. The most important aspect to helps ministry is good communication throughout and good training. If these two aspects are met, the rest will fall into place.

CHAPTER FIVE

* ★ *

QUALIFICATIONS FOR HELPS MINISTERS

All these were descendants of Obed-Edom;
they and their sons and their relatives were capable men with the strength
to do the work—descendants of Obed-Edom, 62 in all.
(1 Chronicles 26:8)

YOU must meet the qualifications of a secular job's requirements in order to get that job. If you don't meet the qualifications, nobody is surprised to learn you didn't get the job. Even though we don't think of it in this way, the same is true in God's Kingdom, especially when it comes to helps ministries. If one is not qualified, one is not going to fit the specific needs of that ministry.

The Scriptures have outlined the requirements for those in appointments, which we know are the offices that oversee helps ministries. By extension, the following qualifications should be things everyone in a helps ministry aspires to see in their own lives. As one participates in the work of a helps ministry, they should see more of these qualifications develop as they grow closer to the Lord through service.

What I have done in this chapter is go down the list of qualifications for bishops, deacons, and elders and compiled them. The reason for this is simple: most of the qualifications are very similar for bishops, deacons, and elders, even though the wording is sometimes different. This is because as offices pertaining to appointments of help, their offices were desired. Not just anyone could come along and receive the position without proper evidence they should fill the role.

Qualifications are important for helps ministries because they prove that helps ministries are important. It is important we understand the Ephesians 4:11 ministry and the qualifications for such; however, understanding ministry does not begin and end there. Qualifications uplift the status and dignity of helps ministries and their offices by proving their importance and standard of minister.

Blameless, of good behavior, of good reputation

People tend to get defensive when it comes to this area of criteria, but it remains top of the list, worded in three different ways in different places. Despite the title of an appointment, a worker must be blameless. This does not mean someone won't have an issue with this person, nor does it mean issues will not arise when people try to cause trouble. What it does mean is that because a helps minister is of such good behavior and such good reputation, there will be no cause to believe the accusations made.

In other words, the Bible is instructing helps ministers to live their lives in such a way that disproves any accusations that may arise. During ministry, when we are help and work with other people, things come up. People get angry, say things that aren't true, or drag up ancient history (things that happened or were done many years ago). The only way to dispel such accusations is to live in accordance with one's beliefs. The best way to live a minister's life is to live without hypocrisy.

Having only one spouse (wife)

This is perhaps the most controversial piece of the puzzle, which is given in the context of the bishopric. Many read the Bible's words about a bishop "being the husband of one wife" means it excludes single people, women, and nonbinary individuals from the bishopric. Is this indeed the case?

There are numerous statements in the Bible that are delivered in what is known as neuter tense – or masculine tense, which is implied to include everyone rather than being gender specific. When the Bible speaks of "sons of God," nobody reads that to exclude women or nonbinary individuals: it's for all of us. Even though it is a gender-specific statement, we do not think it is impossible for those who do not identify as male to become a part of the Kingdom of God.

We tend to selectively apply gender-specific wording as we see fit. The issue of the bishopric is one such example. With the bishopric, one is "overseeing" something – they are fulfilling an assigned duty within a ministerial capacity. Anyone who is responsible for something is "overseeing" it – and, thus, we recognize a woman's ability to oversee matters. This same logic applies to the bishopric, and to all helps ministries, in general. The language is not excluding non-male persons – it was, most likely addressing a marital issue present in that day and age, which we shall speak of momentarily.

The criteria for bishops and deacons' wives were almost the same as for the men, indicating the women held a certain equal status within the community. Even though the statement reads "the husband of one wife," women were not excluded from this conversation, and were to uphold the same standards. It wouldn't be logical to say they were upholding standards if they had no position.

In Biblical times, society was divided by gender. Men and women did not hold the same social spheres, thus meaning the needs church members had were often divided along gender lines. Female ministers – including female deacons and bishops – were needed to meet the spiritual and social needs of women in the community. The infamous "Titus 2 women," according to the Greek, were not just "older women," as our English translations often read. They were female elders, meeting and upholding their qualifications as found in Scripture. These passages do not specifically state the women must have husbands, thus opening the door not just for women, but for anyone, of any status, to serve as an elder in church.

The specific nature of the command to only have "one wife" is not just about men and women – if we take it so literally, it also excludes singles from serving in the bishopric. The issue was not one of whether or not a bishop was male or not or whether a bishop was single – it was a question as to whether or not a man who was a bishop could be married to multiple women. The prohibition here is on polygamy or being married to more than one woman at a time. This practice did exist in both Greek and Roman culture. Women and single people taking multiple husbands was not an issue; thus, it was not addressed. The Apostle Paul was affirming the exclusivity of monogamous marriage among his leaders, not the exclusivity of the bishopric to only married men. If someone desires to serve in the bishopric and they are married, they must have only one spouse, at a time. This means if one is divorced and remarried, they must be legally divorced before they can remarry; if one is widowed, they may also be remarried; if one is single, they may serve as a bishop; and individuals of any gender identity are eligible to serve, given they are not involved with plural relationship partners. Polygamy or polyandry divides someone's time and attention, thus not leaving an individual free to serve in a church appointment.

Vigilant

To be vigilant means to be aware, watching, and alert. Helps ministers must be ready and prepared for any service, always looking for opportunities to be of service. If one is to be in a helps ministry, they must be alert to their task. If a leader gives a helps minister an assignment, it is essential they see the work done to the end, and do it well, alert, and purposed. There is no falling asleep on the job when it comes to helps ministry!

Sober, not given to wine, sober-minded, temperate

Traditionally speaking, Pentecostal, Evangelical, and non-denominational churches were opposed to the use of any alcoholic beverages, even in a social context. Today, we have seen this opposition lax, as many people of such denominational identities believe an occasional drink or glass of wine is acceptable.

It is true the Bible does not prohibit the use of all alcoholic beverages. It is also true the Bible prohibits drunkenness (Proverbs 23:20-21, Ecclesiastes 10:17, Isaiah 29:9, Habakkuk 2:15, 1 Corinthians 5:11, 1 Corinthians 15:34, Galatians 5:20-21, Ephesians 5:8). The commands as pertain to sobriety only have one interpretation: refraining from intoxication in any form. This includes the abuse of alcohol and any other drugs and drinking alcohol while serving on duty in helps ministries. If one does have an occasional alcoholic beverage, they may not drink to the point by which they lose sense of their faculties, nor to the point of intoxication; and a total absence of the use of any illegal or illicit substances whose sole purpose is to intoxicate in any amount, including marijuana and recreational use of prescription medications.

It also includes remaining clear-headed and avoiding things that may cause an individual to become clouded in their judgment or thinking. This means a helps minister must maintain a balance of good health, is not given to chronic emotional outbursts or drama, and does not have a multitude of personal issues that keep them from the work at hand.

Being temperate is often used in common language to refer to refraining from all drugs and alcoholic beverages. The word itself refers to being balanced and not being easily swayed by things. It is, therefore, another aspect of being sober-minded – not giving the mind over to things that will cause a lack of balance in life.

Given to hospitality, lover of hospitality

Hospitality is a long and forgotten art that is also spoken of as a gift of the Spirit (also called ministry or service) in Romans 12:4-6. Hospitality is the ability to make someone feel comfortable, at ease, and, ultimately, like they belong (kind of like being "at home"). It's making sure someone has everything they need to reach this state of comfortable belonging. Hospitality is a personal level of service, making sure the personal needs of an individual are met, as well as those which may pertain to ministerial work. Since helps ministers and ministries are directly involved in serving and giving, it is essential hospitality is a part of a helps minister's attitude.

Apt to teach, able to exhort and convince naysayers

Let me start by saying that not everyone who works in the capacity of helps ministry will be called to continue in ministry and work in an Ephesians 4:11 ministry office. Most people who somehow work in helps will probably never operate a pulpit ministry or some other type of official, public leadership role. This verse doesn't require helps ministers to operate public speaking roles, or public teaching. What it is requiring is the ability for a helps minister to explain what they do, encourage others who do it with them and others in the faith in general, and have good arguments against those who are negative regarding the work and the faith. This means a helps minister should know their faith, complete with some training for such. The help minister needs to be prepared for such because they encounter many different types of people in their work, some of whom will need encouragement, and some of whom will be naysayers. It is to be prepared for the role, in season and out of season.

No striker, gentle, not quarrelsome

The Scriptures are explicitly clear that those who are in helps ministries may not be people who are given to violence or arguments. This means a helps minister must not perpetrate domestic violence, child abuse in any form, abuse or battery, brawling, public or private fights, or given to argumentative behavior. On the contrary, helps ministers are called to be gentle. This indicates an even-temper, proper behavior, and an ability to handle both one's own emotional states and the conflicts which inevitably arise with other people. This is an ability to govern with wisdom, forgiveness when necessary, and without worldly violence.

Not given to filthy lucre, not greedy for money, not covetous

These three phrases all refer to the same thing: not being greedy or moved by money. Helps ministry, as a rule, operates for free. Helps ministries exist to help meet the needs of the church. The purpose of helps ministries is not to pay everyone for doing what they do, but to give those who work therein the opportunity to be blessed by God for the things they do in service to Him. If someone seeks to be paid monetarily for helps ministry, they are missing the point of the work, and the service behind it.

Lover of good people

It is easy to envy the wicked. The wicked seem to have nice things, power, prestige, and do not seem to struggle, as believers sometimes do. That having been said, there are many people in church, week in and week out, who are preoccupied with evil, in all its forms. Their envy has caused them to become fascinated with the lifestyle of the wicked.

This is wrong, on many levels. A minister must be an individual who not only talks the talk, but walks the walk, as well. One who works in helps must have accepted their faith in totality, not in part. The helps minister has the call to make Christianity real – not just a philosophical musing – to those they encounter. If a helps minister is preoccupied with loving evil, they are going to lead those they help astray. It is also important for the helps minister to walk in honesty and without jealousy toward their fellow siblings in Christ.

Just, not slanderers

Being just is a way of living that reflects justice. Justice is the most basic and practical level of righteous living: it ensures that all are considered, and each individual lives in such a way to establish their own dignity without disregarding the dignity of others. If one embraces justice, they do not live contrary to the principles of righteousness in their life. In this way, justice embraces righteousness in a practical way. It allows an individual to invite all people in, without compromising the principles God has established for life.

A helps minister must operate in justice to extend a fair and honest hand to those they will encounter. They cannot espouse views of bigotry, racism, or sexism. They must believe in the power of people to change, and the importance of making decisions based on facts, rather than stereotypes or judgments.

Along the same lines, helps ministers may not be slanderers. This means a helps minister will watch their mouths and the things they say about people. This goes beyond what they say about people personally (although it does include that) into the realm of what they say about people in general, such as epithets, dirty jokes, and vulgar language. The helps minister should guard their mouths, ensuring that what comes forth therein is not slanderous, offensive, or inappropriate.

Holy, reverent

The word "holy" means "set apart." When we look at the commands to be holy in the Old Testament, anything that stood forth for God's service was to be set apart for that purpose. The New Testament reveals that the church consists of God's holy people, a royal priesthood set apart in this generation. The helps minister is called to be set apart for the purpose of helps ministry – dutiful and about the work they desire to do. This doesn't mean a helps minister has to abandon their job, family, or other life activities. It simply means that the helps minister acknowledges their desire to serve, the importance therein, and devotes their Kingdom service to the work of helps. In keeping with holiness, the helps minister should reflect reverence in their lives. Reverence is an attitude which recognizes holiness and respect for the sacred things of God, especially the call of God present in ministers of the Ephesians 4:11 ministry and the work of God's Kingdom.

Holding fast to the faithful Word, as been taught

Helps ministers are not able to have doubts about the Word of God, the Scriptures, or the faith of God. This doesn't mean they can't have questions at times or want to learn more about things, but that their faith isn't in a state of constant crisis. Helps ministries represent the "doing" of the Gospel, as they serve as the hands and feet of Jesus. To realize the relevance of the work, a helps minister must hold fast to the Word. They must understand the relevance of the Word in their lives and see its transforming power to reach others. This command also states being faithful to the Scriptures as one has been taught. This statement also opens the door for additional study, to learn more, grow in the faith, change one's mind, and transform as the years go by. Helps ministers must be influenced by the powerful and life-changing instruction of their leaders in the faith.

Faithful in all things

What does it mean to be faithful? The word itself is "faith-full," meaning, full of faith (the substance of things hoped for, the evidence of that which we do not see). It means one sees a matter through to the end, no matter how things may look in the meantime. When an assignment or task is given, one who desires that task must see it through, no matter how they may come to feel about it in the meantime. This is not only admirable, but also a sign of God working faith and perseverance in one's life.

Full of the Holy Spirit and wisdom

If a helps minister is to be believable, they should be full of the Holy Spirit, or as we call it today, "Spirit-filled." The helps minister needs to know how to serve, where to serve, when to serve, and in what way to serve, at all times. The training of a helps minister needs to return to their mind, and the way it does this stands as they are led by the Spirit. The movement, work, and expressions of a helps minister come forth as they are led by the Spirit, in the work of helps.

Lastly, wisdom is mentioned as vital, specifically to deacons. This was because the work of deacons required special wisdom when it came to distributing funds and goods for the social work of the church. Wisdom is needed in all the helps ministries, as helps ministers operate the good work of church assistance, social ministry, and service. Knowing how to do it and what to do is a powerful gift from God, especially in a position of helps.

When people don't seem to be lining up with the qualifications

The requirements for helps ministers as lined out in Scripture are guidelines. It is important to remember that nobody is perfect. People go through difficult times where things may not seem to be as aligned as we would think the Scriptures demand of them, or maybe are doing better in some areas than others. We put forth our best efforts, do our best, and remember that obedience is better than sacrifice.

The qualifications given need to be taken seriously, but we also need to acknowledge the efforts of individuals as they cooperate with the work God seeks to do in their lives. We also need to recognize and acknowledge the following:

- People have bad days.
- Nobody can control other people. A great helps minister may deal with rebellious children at any varied age, or difficulties with his or her spouse. This doesn't mean the house is out of order, it simply means they are having a difficult period.
- Sometimes a break is needed.
- Sometimes a minister needs to get with God and get serious about some things.
- Sometimes praise and acknowledgement for good service is needed.
- God has made us imperfect, and that reminds us all of how much we need Him. This is as true for a helps minister as it is for anyone in church.

It is also possible a helps minister needs their behavior or issues pointed out and addressed by a leader. Sometimes things have been an issue for so long, they aren't examined in the way they need to be for change to emerge.

A helps minister may be dismissed if chronic issues, distractions, or problems continually keep them from the work at hand. They may also be dismissed for poor attitude, a chronic inability to receive corrections, or an inability to do the work of helps. They may also be reassigned or consider a different area of helps.

The qualifications for helps may seem intimidating, but there is no reason to fear ability or worry you will fall short. Sincere dedication, a good attitude, and a spirit of love and hope go a long way in helping people to measure up, as the Spirit of God works in and through the ministry of helps to encourage and edify in every situation.

CHAPTER SIX

———— ★ ★ ★ ————

UNDERSTANDING COVERING
AND ACCOUNTABILITY

Have confidence in your leaders and submit to their authority,
because they keep watch over you as those who must give an account.
Do this so that their work will be a joy, not a burden,
for that would be of no benefit to you.
(Hebrews 13:17)

I F a helps minister is going to be effective in service, they need to understand the relationship they have to their direct leader, all leaders in a general sense, and the concept of accountability. It is not a secret these concepts are foreign in the modern church, which tends to fall into one extreme category or another. If we are to understand accountability, we also need to understand the principle of covering behind it.

Understanding authority

To understand covering, leadership, and accountability, we must first understand the principle of authority. Throughout the Bible, God gave people (chosen by Him) the authority to lead His people with wisdom and understanding. This is not to say leaders are perfect, but it is to say that those who have been chosen by God (not by human election or selection) to lead are indeed anointed with His grace and virtue to lead. In Matthew 16:13-20, we find an oft quoted verse that seems to cause many to stumble in its understanding. It is, however, the seat of understanding authority:

When Jesus came to the region of Caesarea Philippi, He asked his disciples, "Who do people say the Son of Man is?"

They replied, "Some say John the Baptist; others say Elijah; and still others, Jeremiah or one of the prophets."

"But what about you?" He asked. "Who do you say I am?"

Simon Peter answered, "You are the Messiah, the Son of the living God."

Jesus replied, "Blessed are you, Simon son of Jonah, for this was not revealed to you by flesh and blood, but by My Father in heaven. And I tell you that you are Peter, and on this rock I will build my church, and the gates of Hades will not overcome it. I will give you the keys of the kingdom of heaven; whatever you bind on earth will be bound in heaven, and whatever you loose on earth will be loosed in heaven." Then he ordered His disciples not to tell anyone that He was the Messiah.

We try so hard to define this verse by what it does not say that we are ignoring what it does say. Jesus established a pattern of authority, bestowed in heaven, to those who would be His leaders here on earth. Just as in heaven different orders of angels exist and execute different duties within the authority given, so too do God's leaders do the same thing on earth. Jesus promised that in the Kingdom of God, His right leaders would be one with heaven – and the church of God, His Kingdom, would be the meeting place between heaven and earth. In order to accomplish this, God had to give His leaders governing power, also known as authority.

Each office of the Ephesians 4:11 ministry has its own unique purpose in authority:

- **Apostles:** Structure, administrative order, and discipline
- **Prophets:** Divine order, correction, and direction
- **Evangelists:** Spiritual conviction, guidance, and revelation
- **Pastors:** Empathetic care, tending, and instruction
- **Teachers:** Dynamic teaching, insight, and orientation

Within each office there are also specific examples of those general headings of authority, but I am sure that you understand what I am talking about. Acknowledging the different roles of the Ephesians 4:11 ministry within the scope of authority helps you to understand better how to accept the work and guidance of your leader. It also calls to mind the "keys of the Kingdom of heaven" manifest in these different ministry works. What leaders called and commissioned by God do in their ministries matches the heart and work of heaven. What we allow is what heaven allows, and what heaven allows is what we allow. It is a symbol of agreement and unity with the work and things of God, also showing forth a leader has surrendered themselves to God's work and movement in their lives and ministries.

That having been said, it's vital that you understand the leader to whom you have been assigned. You need to recognize not only their unique gifts in ministry, but more relevantly, the authority and anointing on their life. In keeping with that principle, you must respect the authority God has given them and see the connection between that authority and you as part of their ministry. In serving as your leader, your leader is given responsibility for your spiritual well-being and to do all they can to make sure that you are properly trained and endowed for the different difficulties, pitfalls, and issues that will come along in life.

Covering

The word "covering" as we use it in the modern church is not found in the exact same context in the New Testament. The word, however, is used to describe leadership in a literal sense of being a "covering," or shelter, for those who are led by that individual. This concept is very much in accord with Biblical leadership – leaders of old were often considered as spiritual parents, willing to do anything necessary to train up those they led in the things of the Gospel. I often compare covering to the work of a garment or blanket: it protects, shelters, keeps warm, comforts, and enhances the life of an individual. Covering in the Kingdom of God is no different. When someone serves as your leader, they serve as your covering. This work has both spiritual and practical applications.

Within the Kingdom of God, the offices of apostle, prophet, and pastor are established to serve as coverings for others in the Body of Christ. Apostles cover any office of the Ephesians 4:11 ministry, prophets typically cover other prophets (although they can certainly cover evangelists, pastors, or teachers), and pastors cover other individuals who are not called to a ministerial office within the church. Evangelists and teachers are not covering offices, but rather individuals called to execute a parallel ministry of instruction and education: the evangelist to the non-believer and the backslider, and the teacher to the believer. Neither evangelists nor teachers, are required to have a long-term relationship with those they guide or instruct. Evangelists are accountable for who – and how – they reach, and teachers are accountable for what they teach.

The term "covering" indicates several things:

- **Protection:** A covering's job is to stand as a spiritual guidance and protection. In this world, the enemy seeks to devour the saints of God. The way the enemy may devour can come in any variety of forms. It is the covering's job to protect from such invasions, being aware of the various tactics of spiritual warfare and alert to the prowl that exists.

- **Guidance:** A covering is, before all things, a teacher in the ways of the faith. A leader who cannot teach or train others cannot be an effective covering. A covering teaches in many ways. If doctrine is needed, doctrine is taught. Practical Christian spiritual skills and life application are an essential aspect of teaching. Instruction in leadership, life, and ministry are also essential. A covering also spends time in counseling, one-on-one instruction, disciplinary measures, encouragement, and support.

- **Education:** Even though we tapped into this aspect of covering a bit under the heading of guidance, a covering also has the job of educating those they cover in a manner appropriate to the people involved. For example, an apostle training another apostle is different from a pastoral's practical life approach to the Word, delivered to the pastor's congregation.

- **Leadership:** Covering is indicative of a leadership role. Someone who covers someone else is their leader. This means the person who is covered follows Christ at work in their leader, knowing their leader follows Him. Having a leader does not mean that the leader dictates everything you do in every area of your life, but it does mean that when it comes to obedience on the areas pertinent to your spiritual growth and development and things that may hinder that, you are obedient. Accepting someone as your leader means that they step up and lead you as they are called to do so within their calling, and you receive God's word to you through your leader. Leadership is a fine-line balance: it is a trust of neither abandoning, nor enabling, those who follow. A servant-leader in God's Kingdom recognizes the call and assistance of service, and the importance of growing people up in the faith to spiritual maturity.

- **Trust:** Trust goes two ways. We learn of trust from God, Who we can rely on completely. In a leadership relationship, you should be able to trust your leader. Leaders should never be blabbing or gossiping about your issues, nor should they be gossiping with you about someone else's issues. They also should not walk with an air of judgment or a burdened spirit. On the opposite, as you trust your leader, you should also be trustworthy toward your leader. You should never be gossiping about your leader or exposing personal faults or lapses, judging their decisions, or spreading false stories and rumors. You should honor your leader with the respect you would want extended toward you.

- **Comfort:** When we're young toddlers, the comfort we find in a 'security blanket' is unparalleled. As we grow older, we still find something comforting and secure in the warmth of a fluffy, clean blanket. In times of sorrow or pain, a covering serves to offer comfort and security, and a sense of God's loving, comforting presence during that difficult time.

Your relationship with your leader

Covering is indicative of a relationship. This means that in keeping with your leader, you have a certain relationship with them, and they too have a certain relationship with you. To a certain extent, those who cover are also covered by those they lead, as the two operations serve a dynamic partnership. It takes both the leader and the individual being covered to make a dynamic team. To have a good relationship with you leader, the relationship must be built on honesty, truthfulness, honor, respect, dignity, and godliness. Any other foundation will result in a faulty and problematic relationship.

It is safe to say that most covering relationships today are dysfunctional, rather than functional, relationships. Many situations with a covering fall into extremes: some coverings are extremely controlling, some are extremely lax, and some take on extremely emotional roles with those they cover, becoming a substitute for a natural mother or father. All these extremes destroy the purposed balance of covering relationships and the work of the covering in one's life.

What they do for you

- Bring forth the revelatory (*logos*) Word of God for you in your life, applicable to today's day and time.

- Train and educate in spiritual things.

- Provide guidance and direction in your life.

- Provide counseling as needed.

- Provide an atmosphere for spiritual growth, events, services, and empowerment.

- Provide spiritual services, such as rites, rituals, and ordinances, as needed.

- Offer both discipline and encouragement as needed.

- Protect and defend when something unjust or problematic comes up.

- Model as a good example of accountability.

What you do for them

- Offer service and assistance as needed.

- Defend, as necessary, against attack.

- Walk in a spirit of obedience as relates to directives.

- Show proper respect and honor.

- Watch your attitude with your leader. Be sure to maintain an attitude of humility and good conduct.

- Provide tithes and offerings to the ministry (if your tithes are not paid on time, the Scriptures indicates you should pay a five percent interest for each month your tithe is overdue).

- Do not demand an unreasonable amount of your leader's time.

- Walk respective of the good training and conduct a leader has instilled within you.

- You are accountable to them.

Things it is not your covering's job to do for you

- Make up for the parental figure you do not feel you had growing up.

- Make major-life decisions for you.

- Govern your life.

- Take care of your personal duties and responsibilities, such as baby-sitting or housekeeping.

- Solve problems for you.

- Make sure you are employed, or have personal issues covered for you, such as expenses (rent, bills, etc.).

- Cover ministry expenses for you, if you are in ministry.

- Provide housing or transportation for you.

- Find you a mate, friends, or personal connections of a private nature (doctor, lawyer, etc.).

- Make sure you have everything you want in your life, or give you everything you want.

Accountability

Accountability is the state of being accountable, or personally responsible for one's actions, decisions, and behavior. When one is accountable, they do not hesitate to admit to both wrongdoing and right in their actions. A covering is the person in your life who serves as a source of spiritual accountability for you. In other words, your covering is a person that you answer to when there is a question, problem, or situation that may arise during your spiritual development. Accountability relates to the spiritual, ministerial, emotional, mental, financial, and personal aspects of your life. Even though it is not a leader's job to govern all these areas of life, these areas of life often affect and relate to your ability to perform ministerial tasks and function in ministry. If something comes up and it is seriously affecting your ability to minister, it is your leader's job to bring it to your attention, and your job to rectify the situation.

For example: if a question arises because you've been frequently spotted at bars, intoxicated, on the weekends, it is your leader's job to address this behavior and how it may affect your service in ministry and your spiritual life. A good leader will give the option for discussion and defense and will examine the situation based on evidence and conduct, rather than mere rumors. They will also give the option for the behavior (or conflict which may result, if the situation is based on a lie) to be rectified, with suggestions on how this can be done.

In this context, accountability also relates to authority. As someone who is covered by a leader, you represent and embody their ministry, spiritual work, and spiritual disciplines. If you are somehow misrepresenting their leadership with your behavior, you must be accountable for that in the form of discipline or dismissal. Accountability also means that when you have a spiritual question or a situation that pertains to your spiritual well-being or training, your leader is the one to whom you can go for answers. As you are accountable to your leader, your leader is also accountable to bring forth God's teaching and guidance to you.

Accountability with a covering is only the beginning of what a leader seeks to instill within you. Accountability is something that should exist across the board, all throughout the Body of Christ, and we should always be people who are accountable in church, on the job, in families, and in life in general.

Leaders look for accountability because it is a sign of spiritual maturity. Individuals who constantly blame other people for their actions or the result of their actions are not seen as accountable. Part of work in ministry is responsibility, and part of promotion in ministry is accountability. When you don't do your best, or even when you do your best, and the results are less than what was sought, it goes a long way to be accountable for what has happened instead of blaming someone else. Accountability shows that you are ready to handle the responsibilities that come with promotion, greater responsibility, and greater understanding to tackle the challenges that come next.

Examples of accountability

- Employees are accountable to their employers.

- In twelve-step programs, alcoholics and addicts go through a series of steps that relate to accountability, including admitting they have become powerless over their addictions and making amends to those whom they have hurt through their addictions. Most programs also encourage members to have a sponsor, which is a more experienced member with a longer history of sobriety to help newer members maintain their progress within the program.

- Citizens are accountable to the governments in which they reside, responsible to follow the laws in place and deal with the consequences for disobeying those laws when the laws are not followed.

- Spouses are accountable to one another.

- Children are accountable to their parents or guardians, as these are the people God has entrusted with their well-being.

- Students are accountable to their teachers.

Special circumstances involving covering

When I first wrote this book, I advised against covering others when you're too personally involved with them. I still think this is good practice, as many of us can't handle the finer details required in such a situation. That having been said, I've also spent many years handling some of these special circumstances, sometimes with success, and sometimes with failure. As a result, I think these situations are more special circumstances than entirely prohibitive. Rather than seeing them as impossible, we need to address the issues that might arise in connection with them.

- **Spouses:** There are a few different situations that arise when one is married and in ministry. Both spouses might be in the ministry together or separately, or one might be in ministry and the other not in any form. These three different situations require three different answers to who can cover – or should cover – who.

  First, let's clarify that not every ministerial spouse should be covering their spouse, especially if their spouse is in ministry. Different ministry callings entail different details, technicalities, and needs, and not every ministry is for every person. This is true for a spouse as much as it's for anyone else. Just because ministers work together in ministry doesn't mean one automatically has sway over the other, or that one can effectively guide the other through their unique ministry call. Figuring this out is the responsibility of each couple, especially the longer that time goes by.

  If both partners are in ministry but work in different ministries, both likely need their own spiritual leadership, suitable for the work they are called to do. If both partners work together in ministry, they can have the same covering or different, depending on the situation.

  If one spouse is in ministry and the other isn't, ideally their spouse should be part of the ministry as a lay member. That spouse would, ideally, cover their other spouse, with their membership participation. This doesn't always happen, and if a minister is in a different position than a lay member spouse, the non-ministry spouse may need a different type of instruction, discipline, and assistance that should be sought elsewhere.

Let's also consider that, as spouses, sometimes we need outside assistance that's not connected to our marriage. Sometimes we need assistance from a leader to work out issues they may be having in their personal lives. If a covering is your spouse and they are the person you are having a problem with, or they are too close to your personal situation, you will not receive the help needed to resolve the problem. For this reason, when it is time for prayer in a service, the spouse of a minister should be prayed for by an elder or another presiding minister rather than that spouse.

This is also problematic if one covering the other is of a lesser office than the other. We forget that, as we do not understand Biblical teachings relating to headship, church order is separate from domestic order and that domestic order does not apply in church leadership.

Even in situations where couples share coverings or one covers the other, I still advise leadership support (even in the form of mentoring, friendship, or connection) outside of the ministering spouse. There is no conflict if a minister's spouse desires to participate in the church or ministry in some way under the direction of their spouse, but when it comes time for personal need, counseling, and direction, that the minister's spouse has someone to consult with outside of their marriage relationship.

- **Sharing a covering with a spouse:** Unless neither marriage partner is in ministry (and under a pastor) or both have the same calling, sharing a covering can have its complications. As was stated above, each ministry has a specific vision and specific needs which need to be met through their God-appointed leader. Ministers also deal with personal challenges that may require confidentiality from a spouse or may not require one's spouse to be involved. When both partners are in ministry, it is advisable each has their own covering, to ensure their spiritual and leadership needs are met.

- **Relatives:** When it comes to parents, adult children, or other immediate relatives, covering can be a challenge. It's not prohibitive but does depend on the situation at hand. It depends on the relationship you have with them, how objective you can be for situations and needs, how close you are to them, and the interaction present within that relationship. The pros and cons – the benefits and negatives – of taking on the relative should be examined and, if being their covering doesn't seem to be a good idea…that needs to be said.

I know that for everything I raised here, there may be someone who says they have done what I have advised against, and it has been fine for them. If it's working for you, then you do what's worked for you all these years. This is offered advice, not requirements. Selecting a covering is a drawing; it must be something done by God between the person who covers and the person who is being covered. We need to open ourselves up to God's leading on this matter, even if it goes beyond what may seem comfortable, obvious, or available to us. Whoever God leads you to, that is who you need to have cover you.

Your covering's leader

There isn't much teaching today on the relationship your covering's leader may have to you, for one simple reason: a lot of leaders' coverings don't interact that much with the people who are covered by the leader they cover. Some may have a kind of pass-by-night experience with these people, never really meet anyone or know who they are. Some people never even know who their leader's covering is.

The scenarios above do not depict the proper way for a leader to interact with their covering, nor for the people of God to come to know the leader who educates and trains their leader. For this reason, it's important that we understand the role that your covering's leader plays in your own leadership experience.

The Apostle Paul was a covering apostle. If we examine many of his letters, he doesn't just call out to the leaders – he addresses congregation members and workers within the church, as well (Romans 16:1-23, 1 Corinthians 16:12-20, Ephesians 6:21-22, Colossians 4:7-17). This indicates the Apostle Paul had a relationship based on order with everyone in a church, from those who were in leadership to those who were members. It doesn't mean the Apostle Paul personally covered all those people – we would recognize that is not a part of God's order – but that, because he covered the leadership, he also had a relationship with those who were covered by those he covered.

Your leader's covering should be involved (to the level they deem necessary and appropriate) in the ministry of your leader. They should be actively seeing what's going on, be in communication with your leader, apprised of problems and circumstances that arise, giving instruction and guidance, and participating when it is deemed appropriate and possible.

Because your leader's covering is a leader, they need to be considered and treated as such in all circumstances. You should extend the same respect, courtesy, and good ministerial training toward them as you would toward any leader you encounter. They should always be addressed by title. They should be honored with your good conduct. If a request is made or a directive given, it should be followed, out of respect for their office.

One of the biggest questions people have is: am I accountable to my leader's covering? The answer is yes, but in a different way than you are to your leader. Because your covering has taught your leader, the fruit of their teaching and leadership is found within your leader. This merits a special respect and obedience to your leader's covering. While you don't go to your leader's covering all the time or have the same relationship with them as they do with someone who is your own covering, your covering's leader is a part of your own experience relating to accountability.

It is appropriate to contact your leader's covering in the following instances:

- **If there is a problem or issue with your covering:** If you feel there is an issue with your leader that is not being addressed, or that you are somehow not being treated as deserved by your leader, then your leader's covering is the person to speak with. Depending on the circumstances and the evidence involved, your covering's leader will guide you, handle the situation themselves, or a combination of both.

- **Your covering is either teaching something questionable or behaving questionably:** If you have a leader who is out of order in some way and, to your knowledge, their covering is unaware of the situation, it is important you contact your leader's covering. Please note this should not be done on a whim, an opinion, over a minor disagreement, to get back at your leader for something, or, most importantly, without evidence. Sometimes matters of teaching or even behavior can easily get blown out of proportion when people don't have all the facts or evidence. Your covering's leader would take all matters and evidence into consideration, and handle the situation best based on the facts presented.

- **It's time to move on and you seek to request release from your leader:** The first person you should speak with in this instance is your leader's covering, for one simple reason: there are many reasons why someone seeks to move on from a spiritual situation or person in leadership. It is not the leader's job to try and convince you to stay with your leader but find out why you are leaving. There may be some aspect to their work and ministry that needs further training and examination – and your leader's covering doesn't know that needs to be addressed – unless someone lets him or her know what is going on, and why.

- **Something is going on that you don't want to go to with your covering (at least, not yet):** Sometimes things arise in our lives that, due to our familiarity with our immediate leader, we are not immediately comfortable taking it to them. Whether a personal matter, ministry matter, or discernment about calling, there may be many reasons why we aren't sure how to sort things through and present them to our leader. The leader's covering serves as a great resource to help sort some of these matters out, all within a safe and confidential environment.

When you don't like your leader's covering

As a rule, most people who follow a leader also like their leader's covering, for one simple reason: their leader's covering has trained their leader, and most of the time, both have a lot in common. They are often similar in their leadership approach and agree on key things that pertain to leadership. There are instances, however, where this is not always the case. Just because you love your leader doesn't mean you will always like or agree with your leader's covering. We need to remember that there are many reasons why God draws a leader and a covering together, and, as someone who is under the immediate leader, we may not understand the relationship, nor the reasons for God's purposes within their connection.

I would like to note that this section is not about situations where there may be a very valid reason for disliking someone's covering. If your leader is being abused or mistreated, somehow disgraced, or just a poor leader to your own leader, it is natural to assume you will take issue with that. This section is about general dislike; simply disliking a leader's style, their methods of order and discipline or teaching, or some other general thing that does not relate to abuse, mistreatment, or disorder.

In the Body of Christ, it is to be expected we will not always like every minister we come across. Some people just don't fit our personal tastes, and others have a personality or presentation we don't care for. There is nothing wrong with this, because it is just something that sometimes happens. When it is our covering's leader, however, the way we handle it will have to be different than the way we may handle it with someone else.

Because we are talking about dislike of your leader's covering, you don't have the option to disregard their ministry or replace them with someone else. It's not as simple as turning off the television or deciding never to go visit that ministry again. So, how can such an issue be resolved?

The first thing that must be made clear is that you, as a person under your leader's authority, have no right to question, nor badmouth your leader's covering to your own leader. This is an authority issue, and you do not have the right to spread animosity due to your own dislike. It is also totally out of order to go to your leader and try and persuade them to leave their covering or tell you that they will not stay with your ministry because of your leader.

The first thing to consider is the ministry of your covering's leader. Advanced covering for leadership (such as apostles and prophets) is not the same style or format as covering for the general non-membership of the church (pastors). The way your leader's covering may interact, minister, teach, preach, or handle matters may be very different from what you are used to. You may not like how issues are handled, but that does not make the way they are handled bad or wrong. Because a leader's leader handles issues differently, it is easily to think a leader's covering is being harsh or is harsh or uncaring in some ways. It's very important that ministers are trained in the ministerial differences between offices and in the different gifts and purposes each office serves, to avoid confusion or misunderstanding.

The second thing to consider is that this isn't your covering, and they aren't someone you have to deal with all the time. There is no reason to make an issue out of such dislike, because you are not directly working with them on a regular basis. Whether you like your covering's leader or not is not of great concern to you. All the saved, Christian people you dislike will be in heaven, right along with all the saved, Christian people you do like. You aren't going to skip out of heaven because you don't like someone! Learn to handle dislike with courtesy and tact and stop feeling like you have to like everyone to interact properly with them!

The third thing that needs to be noted: the leader you love has, in many ways, been formed, assisted, trained, and led by the leader you dislike. Your leader's covering can't be all bad if they were influential in the establishment of your leader. Whether you like this individual or not, your leader's covering is still a leader, still entitled to respect within their office, still entitled to courtesy, and still entitled to the ministry protocol that should be extended unto them. Instead of focusing on personal like or dislike, it's better to focus on the conduct that is expected in such a situation.

What it means to be apostolic

Now that we have discussed the basics of covering (which apply no matter what kind of leader you may be under), we need to understand what it means to be "apostolic" and how that relates to covering.

Since the beginning of Christianity back in the New Testament, the church has universally acknowledged something important and relevant about the role of the apostles and prophets in the church. Even when the main church body has been in varied states of apostasy, the church continued to identify itself and its government and belief systems as "apostolic," indicating it wanted to validate its practices and beliefs through the first-century leadership. Down through the ages, even to the present day, the word "apostolic" has been continually used to validate denominational beliefs, whether they were tied back to the first-century church, or not.

"Apostolic" is used to indicate a legitimacy of belief, governing, practice, or both. Most often, the word apostolic is used to refer to two different things, both of which tend to overlap in many ways. Apostolic is, first and foremost, a doctrinal understanding based on the beliefs and practices of the New Testament. This system of doctrine is called "apostolic" because the doctrinal beliefs and practices of New

Testament worship were founded upon the first century apostles. The second understanding of the word apostolic is just as important as the first: it relates to God's system of governmental order for the church, founded on the apostles and prophets, with Jesus Christ as the cornerstone (Ephesians 2:20).

In today's church, the word "apostolic" can be used to mean either of these things, or it can be used to refer to both definitions at the same time. It can be also used to refer to certain denominations, which often have a mix of true and man-made beliefs. Just because a ministry refers to itself as "apostolic" does not mean that it is truly epitomizing the fullness of what it means to be truly apostolic, but it does tend to mean that the leadership is genuinely trying to ascribe to its best understanding of what it means to be apostolic.

It is very important that, as a minister training for helps ministries, that you are a part of a ministry that reflects both apostolic doctrine and governance. In terms of the apostolic governance, which is more of what we are examining in this book, it is important to be a part of an apostolic governing system for your best possible development and purpose in ministry.

When one is in a church that relates to an apostolic order of government, it means that the church itself is built on the foundation of the apostles and prophets. This means the church leadership is covered by either an apostle or prophet. Despite which office the individual who covers the church may be a part of, the offices of apostle and prophet are both recognized and respected for their unique purposes.

It also means that the church rightly acknowledges and understands the role of the Ephesians 4:11 ministry within the church as God's standard for order and decency within church ministry (Ephesians 4:11-16). Not every office of the Ephesians 4:11 ministry has been created for covering, nor is every covering office of the Ephesians 4:11 designed for covering all the other offices or the people of the church. Understanding covering within the apostolic helps us to have a better understanding of the relationship we should have with a leader, and the relationship they should have with their leader.

Within the Ephesians 4:11 ministry, the offices of apostle, prophet, and pastor are the three offices God has established for covering. Evangelists and teachers are not offices that represent covering; they represent a responsibility to harvest and teach souls, and they are important offices; but they do not directly cover people long-term, training them for long-term Kingdom service or ministry.

Apostles are an office of leadership covering, meaning they cover leaders within the Body of Christ: apostles, prophets, evangelists, pastors, and teachers. Prophets are also an office relating to leadership covering: other prophets, evangelists, pastors, and teachers. Pastors are commissioned not to train or cover other leaders, but to cover the general body of a local church, those individuals who are not called to ministry leadership. That means:

- An Ephesians 4:11 ministry leader must be covered by either an apostle (apostles, prophets, evangelists, pastors, teachers) or a prophet (prophets, evangelists, pastors, teachers).

- A pastor covering apostles and prophets is out of order.

- The pastor of a church should be covered by an apostle or a prophet.

- Evangelists and teachers should not be pastors of churches, nor should they be covering other leaders.

- There should not be confusion in the office in which a leader walks. There are no "Pastor-Evangelists" or "Apostle-Pastors," for example. Each minister walking in an Ephesians 4:11 ministry office has one office, and may have additional gifts, which enhance the office to which they are called.

- There is no reason why an individual cannot be ordained for ministry and also appointed in an appointment ministry, as is common. Sometimes someone has credentials as an apostle or elder or apostle and bishop, and while there is nothing wrong with this, the primary identity should be the ministry the individual actively represents at this point, or any given point, in time. Ephesians 4:11 ministry representation always takes precedence over appointment ministry in personal ministerial representation, unless otherwise specified for a specific ministerial circumstance.

The relationship you have with your leader is a powerful combination of spiritual training, guidance, and empowerment to help develop your ministry into all it can be. Whether you will spend your days working in helps ministry or will eventually work in the Ephesians ministry, your leader will prove to be a powerful source of teaching and encouragement for that journey.

CHAPTER SEVEN

— ⋆ ★ ⋆ —

TWELVE THINGS YOUR LEADER SHOULD DO
FOR YOU

But you are not to be like that.
Instead, the greatest among you should be like the youngest,
and the one who rules like the one who serves.
(Luke 22:26)

GOT a leader? Whether you call them mother, father, covering, by title, or their first name, your leader should represent something in your life. Yes, a good leader represents authority and respect, and their office is one to which you are accountable. At the same time, a good leader provides an important element of security to your life and/or ministry. There are many leaders who know how to demand authority, respect, and accountability, but are not doing anything to build up their people. By holding to an exterior appearance of dignity and purpose, they deceive people by having an outward appearance of leadership, with little to no substance.

Being a covering (spiritual leader) indicates a level of grace, protection, and comfort should come from the work of covering ministry. I know that I can be hard on those who are under me at times, because people can be difficult and demanding of leadership. There is an epidemic of selfishness, nasty attitudes, disobedience, defiance, lack of service, and smart mouths in today's church. People desire to mouth off, voice their opinions, and speak with disorder rather than order. Every time the leaders of God establish guidelines for training or membership, someone has a reason why they need to be the exception to that rule. Being a leader can be very difficult. This fact, however, does not change what a leader should be doing for the people they cover. As difficult as things may be, it is even more important to help discover balance and purpose in that call - and step out in faith, being a leader God has created.

Here is a list of twelve things a good leader does - and your leader should be doing for you.

Have your back

Do you feel like your leader is for you? A lot of people have the impression that a leader should be against them, fighting and working in their defense, because that is what they've learned to associate with leadership. Some leaders think the best way to build spiritual character and ministry understanding in someone they cover is to be as hard, controlling, and unrelenting on them as possible. Others think that covering means using the people they lead to build up their own ministries or finances. All of these are wrong, and display a spirit of competition, burden, and an open door for someone to become scared to live, lead or walk in authority (if they are called to do so). While a leader should never be a floor mat or disordered, a leader should also not be the cause of problems in the lives and ministries of those they cover. A leader should never be competing with the people they cover, backbiting or gossiping about them, or causing them to feel discouraged through intimidation. Your leader should be your biggest advocate and someone you can trust to guide you rightly because they seek God's best for you in the Kingdom.

Teach/train you

Depending on your position in the Kingdom (either an attending member not called to ministry leadership or called to leadership), your level of needed training varies. Someone who is not called to ministry leadership can attend service at a church under a pastor and, given the pastor is sufficiently called and meeting with their calling, they will be sufficiently prepared and equipped for living the Christian life. Someone who is called to ministry leadership needs different training, under a different ministry office of the Ephesians 4:11 ministry model, that is more intensive to study in Scripture and equipping for their call. A leader should never take the responsibility of leading someone and not train or work with them in some way. Different life situations, offices, ministers, and experiences in ministry require different training, so yes, a covering may adjust the training to the circumstances - but that doesn't mean training is nonexistent. If you are under a leader who is not involved in any sort of ministerial formation with you...you aren't experiencing the work of a good leader.

Pray for you

This sounds obvious, but you would be amazed at the number of leaders who falter in their prayer lives. In most instances, it's not deliberate. Leaders are incredibly busy as they try to manage several different and special circumstances to function in ministry. Prayer is something most ministers enjoy doing, but life can easily interfere in their scheduled prayer time, whenever that may be. There are also some leaders who believe others should pray for them, but they don't have to pray for others. This isn't common, but it does happen on occasion (and never assume this is your leader's situation). Part of being a covering means keeping people covered in prayer. If your leader is constantly too busy to pray for you, listen to your requests, or discuss with you from time to time, your covering is not doing their job. It is not appropriate for you to pray for your leader and your leader never pray for you.

Take an interest in your life or ministry

Considering the fact that, most likely, your covering also covers several other people, it is not possible for your covering to be at every event you have, every service you have, every life situation that you encounter, or answer every single phone call you make the second you call. Sometimes, some coverings are not able to return calls for several days (and on occasion, weeks) due to preaching engagements, being out of town, or other extenuating ministerial circumstances. It is important, however, that you know your leader is interested in your life or ministry, in what you are doing, and in discussing matters that relate to your circumstance. Your leader should know whether or not you have a calling, what your calling is if you do indeed have one, the name of your ministry if you have one (and whether or not you will be changing your direction in ministry anytime soon), your events and activities, ministry contacts, your gifts and call, your vision, location, and your training, both past and present. As part of your equipping and training, you should provide necessary communication about your life or ministry to your covering in whatever form required - whether it is monthly reports, regular conversations, publications, etc. A good covering is involved in what you are doing, given their situation and yours, when they can. Good leaders lead as servants - by example - as they are hands-on in whatever you are doing.

As a side note to this issue: your covering is not a mind reader. As an extremely busy minister, they don't know what's wrong if you don't tell them. Don't assume they will figure out what's wrong if you grow distant, alienated, or withdraw from participation or communication. The odds are good that they will see such as passive-aggressive behavior and interpret it to mean that you're no longer interested in participating in the ministry with them as your leader. Communication is essential. Communicate your needs and activities to them.

Respect your unique call, life, ministry, or leadership

Not every Christian believer or ministry/minister has the same call, purpose, or work. Not every believer or minister is destined to walk the same walk or do the same things. Some believers and ministers will be married, some will be single, some will have children, some will be childless, some will be younger, some will be older, some will have extensive complications, and some will have simple times. In paralleling the Word, some leaders will be apostles, some will be prophets, some will be evangelists, some will be pastors, and some will be teachers. Having said this, it is important that a covering respects the unique call, life, ministry, and leadership present within those they cover. A covering should understand God's leadership order, whether you are called to an office, the office you are called to if you are called to one, and the ways they can help develop your ministry for that purpose. In understanding this, they should respect the work God is doing within you - not belittle it or demean it. You should never feel like you and your covering are in spiritual or ministerial competition or that your covering does not respect your call, life, or leadership. If you are not somehow living contrary to the Gospel, there is absolutely no reason why your leader should interfere in your life.

Acknowledge your gifts, but embrace your fruit

When we first start in faith or ministry, we are often very enamored with the gifts God has placed within us. A good covering recognizes your gifts but is much more interested in seeing your gifts become fruitful. It may seem at times that your covering is pushing you too much or not pushing you enough, but with a good leader, neither is the case. What a good covering is trying to do is discover the balance needed to help your every gift become productive and fruitful while avoiding extremes. Good leaders want to see you do good things with your ministry work. I know that, as a leader, one of the hardest things for me to do is watch people I cover stalemate in some way. It is hard to hear God tell me to wait to work with them in some area and equally difficult to try and instruct or guide them, only to experience resistance or watch them falter. Yes, your covering is very aware of the work and, if you are in ministry, anointing God has placed upon your life, and is very aware of the gifts you have....but your covering also knows it takes more than gifts to be successful in life and get ministry work done. This is where training becomes vital. If you have a leader who is all about your gifts but not about what you are doing with them or working on doing with them...(insert obvious here).

Make you wait when you need to

When it's about us, we are always ready to go, go, go. Even though we may see the necessity in waiting as applies to someone else, we don't usually see it in ourselves. Nobody likes to hear that it's time to wait, sit down, and discipline ourselves to hear the Word of God to us, for us, and working in us. We don't like to hear that maybe we aren't doing something right or aren't ready for something. A good leader will put themselves aside (and what I mean by that is not hold you back out of their own vanity) and talk to you about seeking God in a deeper way for direction, while offering needed training and correction. If you have a leader who just lets you do whatever you want...that's not a leader who is going to help you grow.

Correct and encourage you

Normal leaders enjoy correction about as much as the recipient enjoys receiving correction - that would be not at all. It is often very difficult for a leader to confront a person they cover with something that is chronically or seriously wrong. Sometimes it gets easier to address the more it comes up and sometimes it doesn't (it usually doesn't), but no good leader enjoys running around, correcting people. Ministry isn't *The Apprentice*. Having to constantly address issues of correction takes time away from other ministry activities, not to mention the countless hours of prayer, consultation, and consideration of how to best handle the matter. It's not pleasant, it's not enjoyable, and nobody enjoys doing it.

The Bible provides an important balance in leadership, however: both correction and encouragement are needed to produce a good leader. If someone is out of line, they are out of line - and that must be addressed. If someone is having a hard time, down, or doing well in their tasks, they need to be encouraged. A leader who does all of one or all the other without finding the needed balance of both is missing the true purpose of leadership and the relevance that both correction and encouragement edify a true leader.

Guide you within accountability and order

Scripture gives us necessary guidelines as pertain to accountability and order. As your first and often primary experience of accountability, your leader should understand their unique role as being someone to whom you can be accountable. We don't often think of accountability as a matter of trust, but in many ways, it is just that. By standing as a voice of authority in your life, your covering should be someone you can talk to about anything, without the fear of judgment. They should be interested in seeing you grow and change, from glory to glory and faith to faith, as you transform and mature in your calling. When you come to them with a problem, a fault, or an issue, a covering should move in correction and provide guidance on how to move past the situation at hand unto a place of truth and restoration. The goal of accountability and order is both understanding one's own position and understanding that of a leader.

Listen

People today like to talk - way too much. Social media, friends, and even members become sounding boards for personal problems. While I believe we should support one another (especially in difficult times), it's not a leader's place to make a member uncomfortable. It is true that sometimes God shows us something or we discover something about a leader, and that in addition to being called into prayer, our leader may reveal to us about what we have discovered. This is different than just unloading a bunch of problems where they don't go. Your covering should listen when you have something to say and offer guidance as necessary.

Provide security and confidence

The callings we have in as Christians and ministers are not easy. Being a Christian means many changes to one's immediate life and circumstance. Being in ministry means ministers face unique challenges as pertain to their office and that can encompass an entire spectrum of different issues. Your covering should be one to affirm your situation or calling (after God has first called you to it) and one who can provide a strong confidence in you as you walk through whatever you must. This means on the days you feel like you shouldn't be a Christian or in ministry, your leader should be one to encourage and shake you into reality, making you realize how important this life and this work is.

Love you

Sometimes people miscommunicate, feelings can get hurt, and things need to be clarified. Beyond this, your leader should walk in love and seek the best for you. The bottom of the whole matter? If your covering doesn't walk in love and display that love toward you, your covering is never going to provide what you need. Granted we all have different expressions of love and ways we show it, you should know your leader loves and cares about you.

CHAPTER EIGHT

$\star\ \bigstar\ \star$

ETIQUETTE/PROTOCOL WITH LEADERSHIP

They honored us in many ways;
and when we were ready to sail,
they furnished us with the supplies we needed.
(Acts 28:10)

EVEN though we don't think of it this way, all helps ministries take on a form of leadership while maintaining a relationship with superior leadership. In a sense, helps ministers are a form of "middle management." It is true that they are not pulpit ministries, and they do not generate as much acclaim or fanfare as other works of the church, but nonetheless, they are about leadership work. Helps ministers are people who, entrusted with the care of service, are working within the churches and ministries to see essential and important jobs as relate to function are completed. This means that helps ministers are very involved with Ephesians 4:11 ministry leadership, other helps ministers, and the general body of the church, all at once. This means how a helps ministry leader interacts with everybody is relevant.

It is especially important to note how you, as a helps minister, relates to those who are in leadership. Believe it or not, how you carry yourself with your leader and other leaders heavily relates to your own experiences in helps ministry. If you seek to be successful in helps, it is important you carry yourself with dignity and respect and extend that to everyone else you work with in ministry.

In this chapter, we are going to look at the proper way to address and interact with leaders. Some of the things in this chapter, you may already know, while some of them may be things you've never thought of before. Whether this chapter proves to be new material or just a refresher course, the information contained will prove to be very useful in your work as a helps minister.

First experiences and impressions

In most ministries, helps ministers are the first individuals a minister of the Ephesians 4:11 offices will encounter. Often, a team of helps ministers (administrative, hospitality, or both) will be in contact with a leader. It is important to remember that, as the first encounter with a ministry, helps ministries leave the first impression about a ministry. This means that, based on an encounter with helps ministries, a leader will either have a positive or negative impression of a ministry and the quality of help a leadership has.

Many people don't take first impressions seriously. In fact, many leaders are told to ignore or "brush off" negative encounters they may have with a ministry, due to excuses. I'm the first to believe in forgiveness and understanding, but we should also never use forgiveness or understanding as an excuse to circumvent accountability. We are a people called to excellence! When we make excuses, a leader is forced to take responsibility for your personal problems and behavior. This is, in no uncertain terms, wrong. Remember, leaders look for and seek accountability, which manifests in this situation as doing required tasks with a good attitude, despite what is going on.

The common theme herein: your problems are not this leader's fault, and it is not your place, nor your right, to dump them there.

- It is not a leader's fault you are having a bad day.
- It is not a leader's fault you do not like your secular job.
- It is not a leader's fault you don't like someone else in the ministry.
- It is not a leader's fault your kids are acting up.
- It's not a leader's fault you are single.
- It is not a leader's fault your spouse is difficult and doesn't like you doing helps ministry.
- It is not a leader's fault that you didn't get your needs met when you were a child.
- It is not a leader's fault that you have trouble budgeting your finances.
- It is not a leader's fault that you don't want to be bothered with the assignment your leader gave you.

Being accountable and responsible means your leader trusts you with the first impression of another leader. In all that you do, it is your job to make sure the ministry is well represented, and the visiting leader is comfortable and needs provided.

Interaction with other leaders

Just because a leader is not your personal "leader" does not mean they are not a leader or that they do not hold authority over you. All leaders hold authority and demand respect, whether they are your personal leader, or not. Even though they are not your personal leader, they are someone else's personal leader, and they are still a leader, in authority, over you. This means they are entitled to courtesy and dignity, no matter whose leader they are.

Different organizations have different etiquette requirements when it comes to addressing leaders. Unless otherwise indicated, leaders should always be referred to by title and their last name or first name, depending on the preference of the leader, when in assembly or group situations. Leaders should never be casually called by their first names without prior permission. Along the same lines, leaders should be approached and handled with respect and courtesy.

Respecting titles, appointments, and offices

What do the words mother, father, sister, aunt, uncle, principal, chancellor, instructor, Mr., Mrs., Ms., Mx., brother, pastor, prophet, apostle, evangelist, teacher, bishop, elder, and deacon all have in common? No, this isn't a great word trivia. The following words are all titles, or terms that relate to the relationship one has with another.

Many in today's church question titles and disrespect offices and appointments. It is a shame that more people do not see the connection between the two. Today we hear debates about whether titles should even be used, or that it doesn't matter what title one wears or uses, because all ministry is the same. If the church was truly where it needed to be, such a discussion wouldn't even be entertained. This proves that the church today does not properly understand, nor respect authority in the way it should.

Respecting and honoring a title shows respect for the office or appointment one is a part of. Referring to someone by title (which is also their office) does not mean that leader is better than you, more important than you, closer to heaven than you are, more favored by God than you are, or somehow intellectually or morally superior to you. What it does mean is that you have respect for the authority God has placed within the church, and you are acknowledging the authority God has placed within that individual to serve in His Kingdom. To be effective in ministry, it is important to stop this nonsense that titles do not matter and that we should not use them.

There should be a continual respect for titles, even when a leader is not a direct or personal leader, or a leader is disliked. This means leaders should always be addressed as follows:

- A leader should be addressed by their title (Apostle, Prophet, Evangelist, Pastor, Teacher, Bishop, Deacon, Elder) and their last name, in formal settings. In some instances, depending on the relationship to a leader, they may be addressed by their title and their first name, but this indicates relationship with that leader. If you do not have a relationship with that leader, you should not refer to them by their title and first name.

- The title a leader carries must be addressed properly. Yes, sometimes we misspeak; but it is important to make sure you address a leader by their proper title. It's a myth that all offices of the Ephesians 4:11 ministry are the same, and that all ministers are just ministers and preachers, so it doesn't matter what title someone carries. The offices of ministry represent different gifts given to the church, and it is important the correct gift is matched with the correct minister.

The following is never appropriate with a leader:

- Calling a leader by their first name only without prior permission.

- Referring to a leader with derogatory speech or racial or sexist slurs.

- Mocking the directive of a leader, especially when given a direct command or request.

- Deliberately calling a leader by a different title because you don't feel they should call themselves by their title.

- Deliberately not referring to a leader by title because you don't believe in titles.

Universal and limited authority

Just because a leader is not your personal "leader" does not mean they are not a leader, or that they do not hold authority over you. Today's church often perpetuates this notion, but that notion is wrong. Just because someone is not your personal leader does not mean they do not have the right to stand in correction or issue a directive. While it is not always wise for a leader to exercise such, there are certain offices by which such is appropriate. It is important that in helps ministries, the difference is understood.

All leaders hold authority and demand respect, whether they are your personal leader or not. Even though they are not your personal leader, they are someone else's personal leader, and they are still a leader, in authority over you. This means they are entitled to courtesy and dignity, no matter whose leader they are. There are also different types of respect, and boundaries that exist within each sphere of leadership.

Within the Ephesians 4:11 ministry, there are two types of authority: universal authority and limited authority. This very simple principle is often misunderstood in the modern church and, as a result, often distorted. Understanding the principles behind universal authority and limited authority helps to better understand realms of leadership and adopted ministerial roles when in a certain setting.

Universal authorities are leaders who have authority in any church, anywhere in the world. Even though this authority may not be always exercised (and it may, in fact, be unwise to exercise it at times), a universal authority has authority that moves beyond the local realm. The way a universal authority may be exercised may be different depending on the office, but the bottom line is that a universal authority has authority beyond a local congregation.

Universal authorities within the Ephesians 4:11 ministry are:

- Apostles
- Prophets

Authorities with a universal scope but without formalized church authority (meaning they are not superior to either leaders with local or universal authority, but run parallel with a different purpose) include:

- Evangelists
- Teachers (depending on their call)

Limited authorities are those authorities within a church setting who have authority exclusively on a local level. While such a leader would be respected and acknowledged as such, they do not hold authority over other congregations other than the one which they preside. These include:

- Pastors
- Teachers (depending on their call)

Understanding the sphere of leadership gives us an idea of how the chain of command works. Even though a leader may not be a personal authority over someone, when an apostle or prophet is present in a church, they represent the superior offices. Their authority, words, and instruction are to be universally accepted, as they are given in proper order. It is inappropriate for a pastor to be giving a directive in a church by which they are not presiding. Evangelists and teachers have the right to correct and rebuke, but do not represent church authority as relates to structure and discipline. It is also understood that these offices operate within the bounds of order, and address specific matters relating to leadership, helps, discipline, and other issues through the proper channels of order, which are those that relate to the leadership already in place.

The appointments and authority

The appointments (elder, bishop, deacon) are also a representation of limited authority, but in a different sense than a pastor or teacher. Elders, bishops, and deacons are only commissioned to do the work for which they are appointed – and that means their authority is limited by their appointment, to when and where they are appointed to do it. It is inappropriate for any of the appointments ministries to check authority over any member of the Ephesians 4:11 ministry.

Inappropriate questions to ask a leader

Once upon a time, people operated by the lost art of courtesy. There were certain questions that were considered rude and inappropriate within certain settings and certain authorities. For example, asking a woman her age or weight was considered inappropriate. Asking a superior about their private lives was considered inappropriate. People did not give graphic details of their intimate lives, and to do such was considered vulgar. Fast-forwarding to modern times, it does not appear that much is off limits. People air out dirty laundry and, as a result, many think it is acceptable – even desirable or considered conversational – to ask leaders any assortment of questions that may be inappropriate.

Today we place great emphasis on the approachability and transparency of a leader. People are under the impression that being an honest and open person means leaving nothing to the imagination and answering every question someone may have about any matter. In keeping with this tide, many leaders have changed with it. Instead of establishing good boundaries of taste and honorability, every and any matter that arises within someone's mind seems to be addressed out of fear.

It is not inappropriate, dishonest, or wrong for a leader to guard their privacy. In fact, guarding privacy is perhaps one of the most important facets of a ministry, especially if it is desired for a ministry to grow. Leaders who run off at the mouth with too much information may find a quick group of people who identify with their situations but fail to hold an audience beyond such. Why is this? Because identity does not equate to being able to be someone's leader. It does not take long for people to start questioning why a leader's personal problems are not solved or getting solved. This leads people to believe a leader's teaching is void of power.

Leaders reserve the right to withhold personal information when asked inappropriate questions (no matter who asks them, even if it is another leader). In keeping with this precept, it is important that, out of respect, certain discussions and lines of questioning are regarded as inappropriate with a leader. Such questions include:

- How old are you?
- What is your weight?
- Why don't you have any children?

- Why do you have so many children?
- Are you dating anyone?
- Why aren't you married?
- Why don't you have a secular job?
- Why do you have a secular job?
- Where is your spouse? Why don't they travel with you?
- Is everyone in your household saved?
- Why isn't the rest of your ministry here with you?
- How much money do you make?

The questions above invade personal privacy and are perceived to try and gain unnecessary and inappropriate knowledge about a leader. When making polite conversation, the following questions are both acceptable and encouraged:

- How long have you been in ministry?
- How did you know you were called to ministry?
- What is your favorite aspect of ministry?
- What is the most important thing to you about your ministry?
- What challenges have you faced in your ministerial work?

Helps ministries service in relation to special events

As we discussed in previous chapters, the world of helps ministry can be very complex within a singular church. While some roles (such as being in the nursery) are straightforward in purpose, it can be tricky to understand how helps ministers are called to step up and serve when a guest minister or special service are in order.

Helps ministries are to be present any time they are called upon for service. This means that it doesn't matter who the presiding minister is; if it is your church being used for an event, any necessary helps ministers should be present for service as directed by your leader. Ministries needing to be present include music ministry, altar work, worship team, nursery, armor bearers or assistants when ministers do not have them, hospitality ministries, audio visual, and beyond, as required.

Being of ministry service transcends your immediate leader and local church. As we reviewed in this chapter, being in helps ministries is about more than just doing one job for the people in your own church.

You will be required to assist with events, out-of-town guests, other leaders, different circumstances, and different people. The better your etiquette, the better you will be able to handle these different encounters as they come along.

CHAPTER NINE

— ★ ★ ★ —

INTERACTING WITH OTHER MINISTRIES

Peace to you. The friends here send their greetings.
Greet the friends there by name.
(3 John 1:14)

I F you work in a helps ministry that relates to work with your leader – such as assistance, altar work, worship ministry, armor bearer, or other type of assistance – you will, at some point in time, visit another ministry with your leader. Many find this experience both intimidating and confusing, for several reasons. The first reason this can be challenging is simple: you are going into a place where another leader holds personal and direct authority, and they may not handle matters via the order you have and are learning in your immediate ministry. They may hold to a different system of operation, understanding, and may approach matters differently. This can leave a helps minister uncertain of their purpose, role, and function in this different environment. It can also be confusing because sometimes different ministries employ a different mode of dress, worship, or authority structure. Sometimes different churches have different beliefs or protocol. In any situation, it is best to be prepared.

Training and preparation

Before going to another service as part of a ministry event, it's important your leader has a meeting with you and any other helps ministers who will also be assisting or attending. Your leader should go over these basics with you, to help alleviate confusion:

- The type of ministry you will be visiting. Is it as your ministry is, or is it different? Does it belong to a denomination? Do they have a different structure or worship style? Whatever it will be, your leader should inform you, so you will know what to expect.

- The type of service this will be (i.e., preaching, guest speaker, ordination, baptism, etc.).

- Necessary attire for the event. Some churches require all present with a visiting ministry to be identifiable by their clothing.

- Necessary materials/items that should be brought for the function of the service.

- Your specific role and function during the event. For example: if a church already has an altar work system and they will be functioning that night, that will mean the altar workers who are attending this service with their leader will either have to work with that altar work team or hold a different function.

- Proper and appropriate conduct for the ministers based on the type of service they will be attending.

Assisting your leader

Assisting your leader in another church or ministry setting is not all that different from assisting within your immediate ministerial home. The major difference is, obviously, the location will be different and the level of involvement you may have may very well be different. No matter what circumstances may arise, your participation, however it will be, will be necessary and important for a few reasons.

The first, and most relevant, is that you know your leader. If you are already working or training for helps in leadership assistance, you know (perhaps better than anyone) how your leader operates, what they do, how they move, how they flow in the Spirit, and what their unique needs are in a pulpit or visitor's setting. You have something to offer your leader that someone else does not, no matter how well-intentioned that individual may be.

The second reason is because your leader knows you. They know the different ways God moves through and within you, and they rely on your spiritual insights as you assist in the work of ministry. Visiting another service, whether it is to minister or to visit, can be a very complicated and difficult experience for a leader. It is easy to be distracted by spirits, individuals who don't receive their anointing or spiritual gifting, leadership conflicts, exhaustion, and the difficulties that involve spiritual discernment and general observations. Leaders need to be able to focus, and your familiar presence is a huge part of their ability to complete their divine assignment, whatever it might be in that capacity. Your leader needs you to pray, to intercede spiritually, to work the altar or assist with other formal ministry works, and to be on the watch for what is going on, as they perform the task at hand.

The third reason is because sometimes individuals who assist leaders in other ministries might be eager to gather around a visiting leader to assist or help, without considering how things may be done differently. Sometimes it will be your responsibility to intervene or instruct in how things should be done, or to make it clear that it is your position to assist your leader, as you are the one who is there to handle those matters for them.

It is your leader's responsibility to outline the needs that will exist, the purpose of the visit, and the situations that you may find, all prior to the service. If you have any questions or are uncertain about what to do, feel free in all things to communicate such with your leader.

Different types of services

Believe it or not, there are different types of services among different Christian denominations and ministerial situations. At one time in history, it was very rare for differing denominations to interact with one another. Differences in beliefs tended to keep groups apart – far apart – from one another. This landscape started to change with the American push westward, as few denominations had efficient enough systems to meet the needs of people in vast areas. Now in modern times, it is not uncommon at all to find various denominations crossing over, sharing similar beliefs and or practices with other denominations, or coming together for different purposes.

It's important to understand the types of services you may attend when an inter-denominational event is involved.

- **Community events:** A community event is one by which many spiritual leaders in a community are called together to commemorate an occasion, pray for the community or nation, or respond to some major news or community occurrence.

Community events tend to be general in nature, hosted by a specific church or community leader, and demand proper protocol and disciplines when in attendance.

- **Holiday gatherings:** Whether it's Christmas, Labor Day, Thanksgiving, Martin Luther King Jr. Day, or the National Day of Prayer, many churches host community events or community-related services for special holidays and national observances. These tend to be much like a community event – hosted by a specific church or community leader – and require the same protocol and disciplines.

- **Regular services:** A regular service is one which falls into the category of a weekly or other regularly occurring service that follows a weekly protocol and form.

- **Special services:** Special services are those which draw people together, including those from different denominational backgrounds. These include memorial services, funerals, weddings, ordinations, dedications, baptisms, and other events that relate to special milestones in people's lives. The protocol, attire, and form for these events varies by the church or ministry hosting them.

- **Conferences:** The term "conference" tends to mean different things to different groups. Some people define a conference as a gathering of denominational churches or believers. Others define a conference as a more general event that opens doors to the community and other groups of believers. In this context, a conference often reflects the beliefs, style, and ideas of a group, while inviting others to attend.

Understanding different forms of worship

When it comes to the expanse of Christian worship, there are three main identifying categories: liturgical, non-liturgical, and Messianic.

Liturgical worship is based around a fixed, established service known as liturgy. Liturgy form is the same from week to week and is based on a responsorial dialogue between a leader and the people. Liturgies typically represent more formal occasions: pipe organ music, hymns, leaders in robes, etc. You will see liturgical form in more traditional Protestant churches that have a direct tie to the Roman Catholic Church, such as Anglican, Episcopalian, African Methodist Episcopal, Lutheran, and Methodist. Some non-denominational churches with ties to one of these denominations may also use a liturgical form regularly or on occasion, such as communion.

Liturgical churches function in what is called the liturgical year. The liturgical year is divided up into different seasons, identified as relates to holidays. The typical liturgical year is as follows:

- **Advent** (Begins end of November/early December; four Sundays leading up to Christmas. Noted by purple or purple-blue vestments [pink on the third week of advent] and an advent wreath.)

- **Christmas** (Begins on December 25 and lasts until Epiphany Sunday, which is typically the second Sunday in January. Noted by white vestments.)

- **Ordinary Time** (Lasts from after Epiphany Sunday until the beginning of Lent. Noted by green vestments.)

- **Lent** (A period of penitence and fasting, which lasts from Ash Wednesday until Holy Thursday, the Thursday before Easter. Noted by purple vestments, except for the third week of Lent, when vestments are pink. Noted by lack of decoration.)

- **Holy Thursday** (Sometimes called Maundy Thursday, it is the Thursday before Easter. It is the memorial of the Lord's Supper, by which some churches observe with a re-creation of the events. Noted by white vestments.)

- **Good Friday** (The Friday before Easter. It is the memorial of Jesus Christ's crucifixion and death on the cross. Noted by red vestments.)

- **Holy Saturday** (The Saturday night before Easter Sunday. It is the vigil watch, awaiting the resurrection of Jesus Christ. Noted by white vestments.)

- **Easter** (Begins on Easter Sunday and lasts until Pentecost Sunday. It is the Easter season, celebrating the resurrection of Jesus Christ. Noted by white vestments.)

- **Pentecost** (One Sunday following the Easter season. It is the celebration of the birthday of the church, the descent of the Holy Spirit on the disciples at Pentecost. Noted by red vestments.)

- **Trinity Sunday** (Observed in some churches [but not all], typically the week following Pentecost Sunday. It is the feast of the Trinity. Noted by white vestments.)

- **Ordinary Time** (Lasts from after Trinity Sunday until Advent, thus a long portion of the year. Many specific feast days may be observed, depending on denomination, in the meantime. Noted by green vestments.)

Major players in a liturgical service

- **Cantor:** The individual who leads the church in responsorial (responsive part-based) singing.

- **Choir:** The group that sings the congregation's part in choral arrangement.

- **Minister:** The leader of the liturgical worship service. May be called an assortment of titles, including "Pastor," "Reverend," "Father," or "Mother."

- **Lector:** The reader during a liturgical service. Also makes announcements.

- **Altar servers or adjunct:** People who serve on the altar in assistance to the minister of a service.

Non-liturgical worship is a little more general in form but can vary greatly in order and style. A non-liturgical worship service is one that does not use a formalized liturgy. What is done in a non-liturgical service can vary depending on the denomination or non-denomination one is visiting. Some traditional Protestant churches use what is known as the order of service. An order of service means the service will be held to the same basic format every week; it is just not based in liturgy. It is composed of hymns, prayers, readings, preaching, offering, and announcements, in whatever order the church or denomination sees fit to use. This type of order of service can be expected in Baptist, Presbyterian, and community churches. In Pentecostal, evangelical, and general non-denominational services, no traditional order of service is used. Most services include announcements, praise and worship (a time for singing songs), prayer, preaching, and offering. Non-liturgical services may or may not involve formal attire or the wearing of a minister's robe, depending on the church involved.

Major players in a non-liturgical service

- **Praise and worship team:** The group that leads the church in praise and worship songs. Often led by a worship leader.

- **Choir:** In some churches, the larger group that sings a choral part behind the praise and worship team.

- **Minister:** The leader of the non-liturgical worship service. May be called an assortment of titles, usually relating to their office or ordination credentials. These can include Apostle, Prophet, Evangelist, Pastor, Teacher or Reverend.

- **Announcements:** Delivered by an individual, announcing the important news of the church or event.

Messianic worship, like Christian services, falls into two categories: liturgical and non-liturgical. I'm giving it a separate heading because Messianic and Hebrew-roots based events are based on a different type of liturgy and non-liturgy than Christian services. When a Messianic service is held, it is typically held on a Friday night or Saturday as opposed to Sunday morning. The liturgy a Messianic service will follow is based on the Jewish liturgy. It is usually based around the Jewish prayer book, with prayers spoken in Hebrew, English, or both. The service also contains Old Testament readings, especially from the Torah. A non-liturgical Messianic service may resemble the Jewish liturgy in some ways, but usually centers around singing, reading, praying, and possibly preaching. When dealing with the Messianic community, it's important to be informed about what they will be doing, what attire is required, and what you will expect – as many of them handle things differently, even from one group to the next.

Major players in a Messianic service

- **Praise and worship team:** The group that leads the church in praise and worship songs. Often led by a worship leader.

- **Cantor:** If the group is more traditionally Jewish, they may use a cantor to lead in song rather than a worship team.

- **Minister:** The leader of the Messianic worship service. May be called an assortment of titles, usually relating to their office or ordination credentials. Most often, they are called either Rabbi or Pastor.

Required attire

The attire required by helps ministers may vary, depending on the church, denomination, or occasion at hand. In the next chapter, we will discuss the specifics of formal ministry attire and when such is appropriate. For this reason, it is very important to discuss with your leader what type of attire is required for such situations.

Differing beliefs and form

It's important to note that, when dealing with different ministries, you may encounter a host of things that are unfamiliar to you. Christianity has spent thousands of years trying to sort out the ins and outs of faith, ministry, identity, understanding, and yes, even truth. If we understand history properly, we understand people have done the best they can with their level of understanding, literacy, knowledge, and historical understanding. This means people did not always get every detail of every matter as always pertains to faith right. Denominations emerged due to the disagreements of human beings, and flourished as people retained the traditions of their founders rather than seeking the truth of faith.

This means modern churches, especially denominations, tend to represent a state of mixed confusion. They will reflect traditional forms of certain things, modern understandings in some ways, and Biblical understandings of others. You may visit a church that employs non-Biblical offices, such as a superintendent; they may regard a bishop as an office like an apostle or use the terms "bishop" and "pastor" interchangeably. You may also see deacons with more power than the pastor, running the church.

Some churches are contemporary in everything but their worship styles. Others are conservative about all matters, including social belief and worship. Some still enjoy modern worship while embracing a mix of different ideas. The landscape is vast and wide, and there's much to learn and see as one ventures out into the world of Christian worship.

Our obvious answer to such is to tell people to abandon their traditional systems, and yes, this may be correct in understanding. This approach, however, has a long history of failure. Moving away from traditions that are ingrained in people's thinking is a process, and the only way such is overcome is through interaction with truth and interaction with those who believe things that are true. This means that, rather than start arguments, it is very important to stand as a witness to truth to others.

This means, above all things, having respect for differences and traditions. Even though you may not agree with what someone believes or teaches, you still respect the right of that individual to have that belief. If you are on their turf, so to speak, you are called to behave with dignity and respect. If they are on your ministry turf, they must do the same. Not every group has the same training, nor the same discipline. The more we learn about the Christian world, the more we learn why avoiding controversies is essential.

The bottom line of it all is to carry yourself as a representative of the ministry of which you are a part. Ask about that which you do not understand and walk within the order God has placed within you and your life.

CHAPTER TEN

— ★ ★ ★ —

MINISTERIAL ATTIRE

"But when the king came in to see the guests, he noticed a man there
who was not wearing wedding clothes. He asked, 'How did you get in here
without wedding clothes, friend?' The man was speechless.
"Then the king told the attendants, 'Tie him hand and foot, and throw him outside,
into the darkness, where there will be weeping and gnashing of teeth.'
"For many are invited, but few are chosen."
(Matthew 22:11-14)

ONCE upon a time, it was easy to get dressed for church. Ministers of the non-denominational variety did not wear collars, robes, or ceremonial attire. They simply wore suits and dresses and embraced very professional attire. When it was time for something church-related, people put on their "Sunday best," so as to bring forth their best for God. Today, it seems like everything goes. You can see someone very dressed in church, or many people dressed up...or the total and exact opposite. At any given point in time, a spectrum of clothing options may be seen in any church event.

If you are confused about ministerial attire and the various requirements, you are not alone. The past fifteen or so years has seen a resurgence in civic and ceremonial attire among many ministers, with a trend toward casual attire among other ministers. When planning to attend an event or participate in something, it can be challenging to discern proper attire. Nobody wants to show up to an event improperly dressed, especially those in helps ministries or who are attending an event as part of a ministry.

Different types of attire

When it comes to attire, a lot of different terms get thrown around today. Many of them are unfamiliar to people, especially in the context of a church setting. Here are the terms as pertain to attire, and what they mean.

- **Formal (black tie):** A black tie event calls for ultra-formal apparel: ball gowns and formal dresses for women, tuxedos for men, and applicable attire that falls somewhere in between for non-binary or gender non-conforming individuals. Formal attire is often seen at weddings, special ministry events (such as balls or dances), or other dressy occasions.

- **Business:** Professional attire based around suits and ties (either two-piece suits or three-piece suits), pantsuits, skirt suits, and dresses. Colors tend to be dark or neutral. Business attire is often seen at ministry business meetings, professional occasions, conferences, and sometimes Sunday services.

- **Business Casual:** Informal business attire that centers around comfort, while maintaining a professional appearance. Business casual includes trousers or slacks, button-down shirts or polo shirts, or knit skirts and tops. Business casual attire is often seen at ministry business meetings, some conferences, and sometimes Sunday services or special events.

- **Casual:** Informal clothing that includes jeans and T-shirts. Casual attire is usually seen in youth or children's events, some conference events, and in some churches, on a regular basis at services.

- **Church:** Formal church clothing that resembles business wear but tends to be more colorful and a little fancier than business attire. This includes suits, pantsuits, skirt suits, or dresses in any color of one's choosing, with matching accessories, such as hats, shoes, and handkerchiefs. Church attire is usually seen at Sunday services, conferences, and special events.

- **Civic:** Civic attire is a term applied to the traditional collar and shirt worn by many denominational ministers. We will speak more of civic attire later. Civic attire is worn only by ministers for specified ministry purposes, which we will discuss later.

- **Ceremonial:** Church attire, usually reserved for formal occasions, that involves robes and garments found in high Protestant churches, such as Anglican, Lutheran, or Episcopalian. It is also seen in some churches that embrace the idea of convergence, or merging modern church with high church ideals. Ceremonial attire is only worn by ordained ministers. We will speak more of ceremonial attire later.

General clothing guidelines

As you are dressing for ministry and church events, no matter what the attire may be, the following guidelines should be followed:

- Whether you identify as male, female, non-binary, transgender, or gender non-conforming, it is your responsibility to learn how to dress for ministry in a way that you are both comfortable with and is appropriate for each situation that arises. In such situations, it is best to have a minister who understands such unique circumstances and helps support you while educating and encouraging you in proper attire for each situation that will arise in ministry.

- When you are in different situations in ministry, attire may vary or change, depending on the requirements therein. Proper advice should be offered for situations in which gender roles are enforced or a lack of protocol for transgender, non-binary or non-conforming individuals may exist.

- What you wear as a minister should reflect the activity you are doing as a minister. Just as the priests of old did not go before God wearing anything they pleased, so too we cannot minister wearing whatever we please. The clothes worn for ministry work while in church should not be clothes worn for other purposes, such as mowing the lawn or taking out the garbage. When planning an outfit, remember the outline above. If you are preaching or ministering, attire should reflect more formal wear; teaching, business meetings, and workshops should reflect business attire; ceremonies should reflect ceremonial and civic attire; and street evangelism should reflect casual wear, just as examples.

- Clothing should typically be matched to the activity at hand, as well. For example, seminars may call for business or business casual, while an evening service may call for church clothing. An ordination may call for civic and ceremonial attire. When in question as to attire, it is best to ask your leader.

- Clothing should not be too tight, too short, too low-cut, or too revealing. Use good judgment when planning attire.

- All garments should be wrinkle-free, neat, clean, and well cared for. Garments should not have holes, rips, or tears.

- When wearing garments that have buttons, make sure the buttons are sewn on and not missing. When wearing attire that contains jewels or rhinestones, make sure jewels and rhinestones are not missing. If they are, replacing them is an easy and inexpensive store-bought fix: get a bag of them at any department or craft store and glue or cement them back on your garment.

- Avoid T-shirts and other garments with graphics, prints, images, slogans, or sayings that are inappropriate or may be deemed offensive.

- Shoes should be matched to the outfit – they should not clash, nor should they be inappropriate to the activity at hand. For example, if you are doing street ministry and the attire is casual, it is not appropriate to wear designer-name stilettos. If you are in church attire, it is not appropriate to wear sneakers. If there is a health reason why certain footwear must be worn, let your leader know in advance.

Civic attire

Civic attire is, in many ways, making a comeback in many ministry circles. Even though it may not be required on a regular basis, it is important to know the basics of civic attire.

It should be noted that the specifics on civic attire may vary between denominations and, at times, even ministries. What is considered appropriate or standard among one group may be totally inappropriate in another. Here we give guidelines, but if there is an instance where specifics are in question, it is best to consult with someone who can provide the specific answers.

The standard of civic attire is the white collar worn by the minister. There are two options for the collar: either a tab collar, which fits inside the neck of the shirt, or a full collar, which is worn around the entirety of the neck. Some traditions forbid the full collar to be worn by an individual who is not ordained as a pastor, apostle, or appointed as a bishop or elder. Iin this instance, a tab collar is required. Others require the tab collar when one is a licensed minister, but not an ordained minister.

There is then the shirt itself, which is worn with a white collar. The traditional and standard colors for a clergy shirt are white and black, which may be worn by all members of the clergy. In travel, black is the traditional color, although any color shirt with a collar may be worn as part of street wear.

- **Apostle:** Red (sometimes fuchsia or purple)
- **Prophet:** White (sometimes royal blue or navy blue)
- **Evangelist:** Gray
- **Pastor:** Royal blue or green
- **Teacher:** Light blue, green, or yellow
- **Bishop:** Fuchsia or purple
- **Elders:** Maroon
- **Ministers:** Black

When dressed in civic attire, one must wear a black suit, one complete with jacket and pants or a skirt. Many denominations and church associations require women to wear a skirt of appropriate, below-the-knee length when in civic attire (they forbid or frown on women wearing pants when in civics). Exceptions to wearing a skirt are social activism, justice, or work done outside of the church. In such instances, black dress pants are a must. Pants require black socks and shoes, and skirts, black pantyhose and formal dress shoes. Jewelry should be kept to a minimal, except for a silver or gold cross, worn with a specific color cord (that should be specified by the ministry).

Ceremonial attire

Ceremonial attire varies depending on the church or ministry you are dealing with. It also varies depending upon the event at hand. Ceremonial attire can be very simple or very elaborate. Below are some of the basics of ceremonial pieces and what they are.

- **Cassock Robe:** A basic preaching robe that buttons up the front and is worn like a long jacket. Cassock robes are worn for preaching or for more formal events by those who are not much for robes on a regular basis. They come in a variety of colors and styles.

- **Chasuble:** The outer garment worn in a formal setting that slips over the head and is free-fitting on both sides, without sleeves. They come in many colors and match the liturgical season or feast color of the day.

- **Alb:** The plain white garment worn as the base of all formal ceremonial attire in liturgical circles.

- **Cincture:** A rope band worn around the waist of an alb.

- **Stole:** A colorful and embroidered scarf that hangs around the neck and down the front of the body, usually fringed at the end. It is worn under the chasuble.

- **Prayer shawl/mantle:** A garment for prayer worn wrapped around the shoulders and back, meeting in the front of the body. A prayer shawl may represent a traditional Jewish appearance, with the fringes and Hebrew lettering, or may be knitted or modern, made to represent more of a modern interpretation of the garment.

- **Mitre:** The large hat worn by a bishop in liturgical churches and, in some circles, an apostle.

- **Yarmulke:** The small pink or red skullcap worn by Jewish men and sometimes Messianic adherents.

- **Cope:** the outer-cape worn to match the liturgical cassock worn by a minister. Traditionally used for outdoor functions.

When civic and ceremonial attire are appropriate

Most ministries do not require their ministers to be in full civic attire for regular services, conferences, seminars, or general events. Civic and ceremonial attire are usually reserved for ceremonial occasions, such as dedications, communion, weddings, funerals, and ordinations. Even in these instances, civic attire may not be required according to every group or polity.

Civic attire is never appropriate for daytime seminars, forums, or other events that are centered around academic events.

The call to wear white

In traditional Pentecostalism, wearing white was considered customary to formal civic and ceremonial attire. This was especially true for female preachers and ministers. In some ministries, white garments (suits, dresses, plain robes, etc.) are considered formal ministerial wear and more customary than wearing the formal ministerial attire. When called to wear white for an event, it is inappropriate to think civic attire or ceremonial attire can serve as a substitute – one must show up wearing white. In keeping with this, the attire should be pure white – not off white, ecru, beige, or darker shades. White is used to represent purity in Christ, redemption from sin, and echoes the principle of being dressed in white by God in the last day.

Garments every minister should have

The following is a list of garments every minister should have to be fully prepared for all duties at hand.

- At least one church suit and dress (for those who identify as female) for ministering on church occasions
- At least one business suit of a dark color for business attire occasions
- At least one outfit that can be considered business casual
- One black cleric's collar shirt with tab collar (for evangelists, teachers, ministers, elders, deacons) and one full collar (for bishops, apostles, prophets, and pastors)
- If in an Ephesians 4:11 ministry office, the necessary color cleric's collar shirt

- Both a tab collar and a full collar
- One basic black suit, with either pants or a skirt
- Basic black socks (for pants) or pantyhose (for skirts)
- Black dress shoes or black pumps
- One basic cassock robe in a color to be determined by ministry or necessity (recommended color: black)

CHAPTER ELEVEN

--- ⋆ ★ ⋆ ---

MINISTER'S LICENSE AND ORDINATION

Then Moses said, "You have been set apart to the LORD today,
for you were against your own sons and brothers,
and He has blessed you this day."
(Exodus 32:9)

D O you need a minister's license? What does having one mean? What is the difference between license and ordination? Are they required for ministry? If you are in helps ministry or are training for Ephesians 4:11 ministry, these are questions you probably have about minister's licenses and ordination.

There are a lot of rumors and beliefs as they apply to both today. Some people insist ordination and licensing are not necessary, while others will not allow someone to preach without either, or both. For the helps minister or up and coming minister in an Ephesians 4:11 office, it can be a confusing process of discernment to know what is needed, and why.

Here we are going to dispel the confusion about licensing and ordination, and understand why each is important to the minister, depending on their calling and purpose.

What is a minister's license?

A minister's license is a certification for qualified ministers, issued by another ministry organization, both of which hold licensure and charitable status within their immediate domicile. In other words, a minister's license is a certification, issued upon certain qualifications, that entitles the minister to perform certain duties that have legal as well as spiritual significance.

A minister's license is not a requirement for pulpit preaching (sometimes this varies, but one is typically not required to preach in one's own church or churches within one's locale), street preaching or witnessing, teaching on the local level (as long as such instruction is not for a license or ordination), or the volunteer works of the church, such as working in the nursery, tending to the building, or other works that do not involve formal ministerial work. A minister's license, often specific to include the works necessary to the office, legalizes the bearer to officiate the following actions:

- Baptism
- Communion
- Weddings
- Funerals/home going
- Ordinations
- Establish a church or ministry on the legal level

A minister's license may be issued as necessary for anyone who is in the Ephesians 4:11 ministry or in the work of the appointments. It is verified by a raised seal, complete with signatures, dates, and terms of the license. A minister's license may be temporary (only given for a season, while someone fulfills an appointment) or permanent (accompanied by a ministry ordination).

How do I know what my minister's license entitles me to do?

Most minister's licenses specify what the bearer of the license is allowed to do, in accordance with their calling and under the governance of that ministry. They are generally very specific and written to specify the ministerial needs of both the governing organization and the minister receiving the license. It is important that the terms of a minister's license are clearly understood prior to any actions as a minister.

What is ordination?

Ordination is the certification and ceremony by which a minister in the Ephesians 4:11 ministry is officially and legally commissioned to do their work of the Gospel. It acknowledges the call of that individual, by God, to work in their purposed office. It is both a spiritual and legal acknowledgement of the ministry work, sealed with by the laying on of hands.

- **Affirmation:** Apostles are affirmed to their office, as it is a confirmation of God's call and sending forth in their lives.

- **Mantling:** Prophets are mantled, signifying the prophetic mantling and seal upon their lives.

- **Commission:** Evangelists are commissioned to preach the Gospel.

- **Installment:** Pastors are installed to their local congregations, to remain there and shepherd the flock.

- **Appointment:** Teachers are appointed to teach the Word and bring forth instruction on God's revelation.

Ordination is typically marked by both a ceremony and a certification, which is the legal requirement for an ordination to stand as valid. Ordination establishes (as is clarified on the certificate) what a minister is specifically allowed to do within the parameters of their ministry office. It is verified by a raised seal, complete with signatures, dates, and terms of the certification. Ordination is not, as a rule, something that is temporary or done on a temporary basis. There are, however, circumstances where an ordination or minister's license can be revoked.

Why aren't appointments ordained?

As was stated earlier, the ministry of appointments (deacon, elder, and bishop) are licensed and/or ordained depending on need. As these works oversee helps ministry, they may or may not require ordination or licensing for their work. These positions are a desired service, not a divine call. If they won't be doing anything that requires a license or ordination, there's no reason to do either one.

When a license and ordination can be revoked

It used to be rare for a minister's license or ordination to be revoked and was considered an extreme disgrace for such to happen. Having a minister's license and ordination revoked was akin to being disfellowshipped (excommunicated) and disgraced. It used to be almost impossible to be reinstated or find another organization by which to practice ministry, especially if the issue somehow related to personal misconduct.

Ministry licensure and ordination revocation are usually done for one of three reasons. The first is because a minister desires to leave a fellowship or denomination. Generally, licensure and ordination are non-transferable between groups. If someone no longer desires to be part of an organization or under the fellowship of a leader, their credentialing is often pulled, freeing them to find what they need with another organization. In such an instance, it is not a stripping or disfellowship, but a parting of ways and ideals that are found to be irreconcilable. In most modern instances, this is probably the most common reason why a ministry license and ordination are revoked. Unless a leader states such stands in the face of departure, papers are invalid when a minister decides to move elsewhere.

The second reason license and ordination may be pulled is because it shouldn't have been done in the first place. Minister's licenses and ordinations are given at a leader's discretion, and there are often clauses as to why it is given. It may be given from a "review of credentials," "review of qualifications," "review of Christian lifestyle," "Biblical views or doctrines," "completion of training program," or a combination of all the above. Sometimes leaders issue credentials when someone's views conflict with their understanding of the above criteria, only to discover this when issues or conflicts arise in the house. As a result, to maintain the order of an organization, papers may be pulled. When this happens, a minister should resign rather than face dismissal.

The third reason relates to the second point. The clauses clearly stated on license or ordination certificates give an overseeing organization the right to revoke if they feel that, in any of these areas, a minister has somehow faltered, changed, or is not aligning with the upholding of such desired standards. Of the three situations, this is probably the least common. Leaders and their organizations don't tend to issue ministerial credentials arbitrarily, so they aren't usually removed arbitrarily, either.

The reality of this, however, is that even though license and ordination can be revoked for any reason, it should not be. The three reasons above outline the need for caution and discernment when it comes to issuing such rights. Licensure and ordination should be revoked as necessary, where a minister is no longer in alignment with necessary standards or has fallen into a state where they can possibly disgrace the ministerial office. If someone decides to move on, they should do so, recognizing and understanding the realities therein.

Along the same lines, depending on the wording of a license, a minister's license may expire. This is different from a revocation. When a license is given for a period, it simply means the license is expected to be in use for that time, but a time will come when it is no longer needed. Expired licenses can be easily renewed, as needed.

Can I just get a minister's license on the internet?

Even though there are organizations which sell minister's licenses online, it is not the same as being granted one by an overseeing, federally recognized ministry that you have a relationship with and can verify your work. Even though online licenses may sound like an easy fix, they often limit what one is able to do and are considered invalid in many church and ministry circles. They are also not acknowledged in all states or countries.

Qualifications for license and ordination

The qualifications to receive a minister's license or be ordained often vary according to the ministry that is issuing such. Some require extensive training, while others do so after one has spent a period of time in a helps ministry or some sort of ministry service. General requirements typically include both a period of training and educational study.

Reasons licensing and ordination are important

In our current world, anyone can put up a website and pretend to be something they have no credentials or authority to be. If anyone spends time on social networking sites such as Facebook, one can truly see why licensing and ordination are important. People of all varieties of backgrounds claim to be one thing or another and insist God has appointed or ordained them to whatever it is they are doing.

This kind of ministerial approach represents disorder. God is not about confusion, nor is He about disorder. We know the Word clearly tells us to submit to the governmental authorities put in place to maintain order. Having a minister's license and proper ordination as necessary are a sign of respect for authority, order (both spiritual and secular), and good sense. Trying to skip over both are a sign that someone is out of order and missing God's purposes for them in life.

CHAPTER TWELVE

———————— ⋆ ★ ⋆ ————————

ASSISTING WITH MINISTRY EVENTS

Commit to the LORD whatever you do,
and He will establish your plans.
(Proverbs 16:3)

W
HEN it comes to event planning, helps ministers are essential to the planning process. From arrangements to assisting with the event itself, helps ministers are often involved in an event from start to finish. In many instances, helps ministers become an important and reliable aspect of any ministry, especially when a leader can rely on faithful and stable people to assist as needed.

Throughout this chapter, we are going to look at events and some common duties assigned to helps ministers when it comes to ministry event planning. Learning about this aspect of ministry can be challenging at first, but many of these skills are important to learn and know for life and ministry work in general.

What is an event?

An event is any ministry activity that is outside the regularly scheduled services and activities. Unlike regular services and activities which tend to involve the members of a ministry, an event seeks to draw believers, non-believers, community members, or all of the above to that event. It is a special occasion that transcends the immediate people who may always be a part of things, reaching out with a special theme or occasion.

With this understanding, examples of an event include:

- Special interest conferences
- Community service

- Healing service or deliverance service
- Special guest speaker
- Theme conference event
- Arts event
- Revivals

The basics of events

Whenever you are doing an event for the first time, the purpose of that event is to introduce your ministry's unique vision (as pertains to the event) to an area or region. It doesn't matter if you've done this specific event a million times somewhere else, or that you have done other events within this area or region before. Every time you do something new, you are doing it for the first time; with every new event, you are starting again. The second time you hold the same event it is to re-introduce the event. The third time and beyond, it is to expand and grow the vision, wherever you do it.

The expense of conference hosting

Most leaders who have hosted an event understand the expense involved. When planning a new event, it is very easy to misjudge the anticipated cost. When planning an event, leaders should have an expense account or a fund account for events, to ensure all expenses will be financially covered without debt or burdens on helps ministers. As a minister, you should never be put in a position to cover your church's event, unless you are the one who is hosting it. Events should be financially planned as much as following a leader's vision for that event, and finances should be duly considered.

Everyone with a job to do

Everyone who is in helps ministries should have a job to do, falling within the parameters of their ministry work description, when it's time for an event. Events do not come together without intense teamwork and preparation. Even though an event's purpose is to draw people who may not normally be a part of the regular ministry work, it takes the assistance of regular helps ministry workers to bring an event to pass.

Leaders should schedule meetings with helps ministers every so often in order to ensure the ministries are functioning well, without a lot of headache or issues. During such meetings, scheduled events should also be discussed, as in keeping with needed helps ministries for the event and who will be doing what in preparation of the event. Your purpose in the event should be very clear and understandable to you, with the option for good communication and information to be made available as it arises.

The four keys to good event planning

Good events do not just happen. They are the result of sound thinking and good planning. There are four main keys to good event planning:

- **Good advertising:** Good advertising involves more than putting up a Facebook status or making an all-text flyer in Microsoft Word. Good advertising is a combination of using all available options to get the word out about an event. The following components are involved in good advertising:

  a. *A solid flyer that can be used both for printed distribution and for digital distribution through online social networking sites:* It should be eye-catching and include all vital information that includes photos of speakers or hosts, event location with address, contact information (including a phone number), room block information, event dates, times, and any other vital information for the event itself.

  b. *Public service announcements on radio, television, and newspapers:* Public service announcements are free news bits for non-profit organizations that give the organization the opportunity to promote their event. Most public service announcements must be kept short, only to the immediate and required information, and must be received by the radio station, public access channel, or newspaper within two to six weeks prior to the event. For more information on how to submit a public service announcement, contact your local stations. Many times, they provide a form.

  c. *Internet distribution:* The internet is the great telephone pole of the world, giving ministries the ability to promote their events to many people in diverse areas for little or no cost.

Never underestimate the value of Facebook statuses, promotions, events, and other social networking opportunities to expand the opportunities for people to hear about your event.

    d. *Word-of-mouth:* Most people in the church world still attend events due to the recommendation of someone they know. Tell others about the event! Get the word out! Let people know what you are doing and encourage them to attend!

- **Positive word-of-mouth:** As I said above, word-of-mouth is still the best way to advertise a ministry event. Get the word out about what you are doing!

- **Solid venue:** Having to change a venue multiple times makes people leery about attending an event. It's important to know where you are having an event and when for advertising purposes. A venue can be a church location, another church location, a hotel conference room, a conference center, a civic or community center, or other available location suitable for your event. Solid venue is a sign of solid vision and gives attendees the assurance that this event has been considered from every angle.

- **Plenty of time to advertise:** When it comes to events, give yourselves at least a three-to-six-month advertising span of time to spread the word. Longer time to plan an event means more people who are aware of it and able to plan to attend.

Planning for guest speakers

Helps ministers are usually given the task of making arrangements for guest speakers for events. This is a big task, and one of the most important when it comes to event planning. If a helps minister drops the ball on this job, it can make for a disaster event.

    When assigned this task, your leader should go over the basics you will need to know. These basics include:

- Any information they have on the speaker, especially as pertains to honorarium.

- The dates the speaker will be speaking, and when they will be coming in and when they will be departing.
- Special requests, or special circumstances, if any exist.

After discussing with your leader, you should contact the guest speaker to obtain all necessary information to help book hotel, travel, and meet with honorarium requirements. Questions you should ask include:

- Honorarium specifics (if you do not know)
- Nearest mode of travel for them (airport, train)
- Specific times of day required for departure or return
- Special requests, if any
- Any direct questions as guided by your leader

Hotel booking

If you are given the responsibility of booking a hotel for an event, you are responsible to do the following:

- Find the best option to fit the ministry's needs for the best price.
- Reserve all necessary conference rooms and private rooms for speakers.
- Reserve a conference room, if needed.
- Set up a conference room block, if needed.

The best way to book a hotel is to obtain a list of local hotels and make some inquiries about which one has the best deal for your needs. I recommend local churches create a series of directories with relevant regional centers for events and other projects, so ministers have easy access to essential information. Most hotel personnel are extremely friendly and willing to work, assist, and provide information as needed. If you are gathering the information, take it to your leader for the final decision. If you are assigned to book the rooms, you should be provided with a church or ministry credit card with which to do so. You should never use your own private means or credit card to book or reserve rooms for a ministry event.

Room blocks

A room block is when a hotel sets aside a certain number of rooms for a period as a complimentary service to generate business for that hotel. When a room block is requested, a hotel reserves a certain number of requested rooms at a certain special rate for guests. These rooms are available at that rate for the duration of the event, usually as stipulated by the one who makes the room block. People can reserve a room for part or all the nights of the block. That room block typically remains for up to so many weeks before an event, requiring those who desire to reserve for it to book in advance, by calling the hotel directly. When calling for a room block, people should request the room block name – which is typically the name of the event. For example, a Sanctuary Apostolic Fellowship Empowerment Ministries event would have a SAFE Ministries room block.

Booking tickets

Booking tickets is often considered one of the most confusing aspects to event planning, but it can be one of the easiest if you know what to do and where to start.

When booking an airline ticket, the most pertinent information is the airport which one departs from and the airport where one will arrive. When you have this information, the rest comes along easily.

It is fine to use general search sites that we see advertised on television to get an idea of what an airline ticket may cost for a trip. It is inadvisable, however, to use these sites to book the ticket. When booking a ticket, use the airline's website directly. Also avoid booking a hotel and airline together through those television-advertised sites, because there are often many hidden conditions that can complicate or interfere with travel. Prices are usually the same, and you have more options when purchasing the ticket. You are also able to avoid complimentary booking fees that some of those sites charge. Booking directly through the airline's website ensures you have full access to the information you need for that ticket, no surprises or hidden fees, and that you can contact them as needed. Keep in mind the following:

- Domestic flights are best booked at least 38 days before your trip, and international flights at least 60 days before your trip.

- Airlines often charge fees for checked baggage, so it is good to know how much they charge per bag (or if they do not charge for baggage at all), in case you are asked.

- Pay close attention to when a plane departs and when it will arrive, to leave no one waiting at the airport. Also pay close attention to when a plane departs for a guest to return home, to make sure they are at the airport in plenty of time.

- Make sure a ticket is forwarded to the appropriate individual, with at least a few weeks' notice for trip preparation.

When booking a train ticket in the United States, one visits amtrak.com and pays for the trip, on that website. As a rule, train tickets should only be booked upon request, if indeed someone has a reason why they are unable to fly. Most of the time, train tickets are just as expensive as airfare but can cause significant length to a trip and inconsistencies in arrivals and departures. When travelling overseas, trains are one of the most common methods of travel and are often required for getting from one place to another.

When you are asked to assist your leader with travel for an event

There may be times when a leader either asks you to accompany them to an event or you offer to attend an event with them. When a leader is being invited to an event as a speaker, the above rules are standard – only the work and operations would be done by the inviting ministry.

The arrangements for your trip sometimes vary according to ministry operations. If your leader is the one who is speaking, the inviting ministry is only responsible for the travel and accommodations for your leader – not for you. Sometimes ministries may cover the expense for someone to travel with the leader, but this is more of the exception than the rule. If your leader is not speaking and you are simply attending an event with them, the travel costs are at the discretion of you and your leader. If you are the one who offers to see your leader's way, then this means you are responsible for both your costs and your leader's costs.

Events can be a lot of work, especially for the assistance of helps ministries. The product of a ministry event, however, can be one of the most rewarding experiences a helps minister experiences. Teamwork, support, encouragement, and hard work all function together to bring forth an atmosphere where the Spirit can move and empower the lives of others as His workers come together in His grace.

CHAPTER THIRTEEN

— ★ ★ ★ —

GENERAL PRECEPTS FOR GOOD HELPS
MINISTRY OPERATIONS

In the same way, you who are younger, submit yourselves to your elders.
All of you, clothe yourselves with humility toward one another, because,
"God opposes the proud
but shows favor to the humble."
(1 Peter 5:5)

THROUGHOUT this book, we've looked at many different aspects of helps ministry, from procedure and protocol to dress, etiquette, and event planning. In this chapter, we are going to look at some general precepts that can help create balance and focus in your work as a helps minister.

Being connected to the Body of Christ

Because helps ministers tend to work with leaders, it can be tempting to spend and devote all your time in church and in faith matters to your leader or leaders. Never forget, God has placed you within a body of believers, His Body of believers! There are more people in the church than just your leader. Yes, it is important to attend to the work you have been assigned, but God has also called you to fellowship. Do not ignore others in the church in favor of leader exclusivity or the exclusivity of those you are working with in your helps ministry.

Service attendance

Part of being connected to the Body means being a part of the various works and functions of the church or ministry of which you are part. Attend services any time you can – not just when you are scheduled to serve or do something ministry-wise. It says a lot to your leaders when you are a part of the church beyond the ministry work you are doing. It truly shows that you know God has commissioned you to be there, at that point in time, and are committed to the work God is doing in that place.

Punctuality

Being on time is a major problem today. We are late for work, church, school, events, and our own planned outings. It has become so commonplace for people to be late, it is often just expected. Punctuality is a sign of respect for other people's time and a sign that you respect yourself enough to be where you are needed when you are needed there. A helps minister who is chronically late is a helps minister who will never be promoted.

Courtesy

Attitude is essential in helps ministry. When dealing with everyone you encounter – from those you assist to your leaders – having a good attitude makes a marked difference in the perception of both you and your work. Using the basic guidelines of being polite, listening when spoken to, obeying when given a command, and being kind in speech and behavior to others goes a very long way when dealing in helps ministry.

Listening

It amazes me how little people listen in our modern times. With a great eagerness to be heard, people disregard instruction and attentiveness. This affects one's ability to be obedient, not to mention, it shows great disrespect. When you are being spoken to, listen. If clarification is required, request such and get the information needed to continue the directive. Don't blow off or ignore those who are speaking to you.

Ministry representation

As a helps minister, you are representing three different aspects of ministry: the ministry you are a part of, the helps ministry you work in, and your own ministry. This means wherever you go, you are representing your leader, your helps ministry work, and yourself. Keeping this fact in mind helps to center your focus and realize that people are watching what you do as a living witness of the Gospel.

Humility

Arrogance is unattractive in a helps minister. Working in helps ministry for attention or glory may produce that immediate fruit, but will be cast down in the long run. If you are called to do a work of assistance, it should be done with humility, love, and grace, rather than competition and arrogance. Leaders truly dislike complaints of bad attitude, glory-seeking, and attention hounds – because they are all signs of complete immaturity and abuse of ministry positions.

Produce fruit in the ministry

No matter the task, the goal of completing any task is to bring forth productivity (fruit) from it. If you are working in helps ministry, you are called to produce fruit from that ministry. This means you do the absolute best job you can with this assignment. Whether nursery or street ministry, leadership assistance or altar work, or any and all of it in between, do the very best you can with focus and discipline to the ministry at hand.

Attend to the ministry work at hand

It is true that some in helps ministry will move on to work in the Ephesians 4:11 ministry. If that is your situation, then we praise God for the call on your life. Even if that is where you know you will be one day, you must realize that God has called you to helps for the time being – and keep your focus there. Right now, you are called to do exactly what you are doing, and contentment where you are is a powerful thing. Focusing on where you think you will be one day in the future is not going to help you right now. If God has you in helps for this time, you are there to learn something that will benefit you both now and later. Seeing this can give you a focus for where you are on the way to where you will be.

CHAPTER FOURTEEN

———— ⋆ ★ ⋆ ————

TEN REALITIES OF MINISTRY YOU NEED
TO EMBRACE TO RUN YOUR RACE

*This service that you perform is not only supplying the needs of the Lord's people
but is also overflowing in many expressions of thanks to God.
(2 Corinthians 9:12)*

IT'S no secret that when I started out in ministry over two decades ago, I didn't have the first clue of what I was doing. I knew little about ministry, how it operated, or that it had a day-to-day function. What I did know about ministry and its protocols and functions quickly changed within a few years of starting ministry work – and would go on to change again and again as different standards and concepts of what it means to be a minister continue to change in today's world. Nowadays I hear every demand, from first-class tickets to limousines, to five-star hotels and restaurants, to ten armor bearers established for "service!" Then we have the extremes of ministers who refuse to ask for anything, even travel expenses, because they believe they don't have the right to request anything. Both extremes reveal a deeply confused concept of ministry but expose something deeper: the fact that many have no idea of the realities of ministry and the complications that ensue as a result.

It seems today as if everyone in the world thinks they are called to ministry. I use the term "thinks" because statistics cite an overwhelming majority of those who think they are called into ministry won't last more than two to three years. How do those of us make it who are truly called? We embrace the Apostle Paul's words in 1 Corinthians 9:24-27:

*Do you not know that in a race all the runners run, but only one gets the prize?
Run in such a way as to get the prize. Everyone who competes in the games goes into
strict training. They do it to get a crown that will not last, but we do it to get a*

crown that will last forever. Therefore I do not run like someone running aimlessly; I do not fight like a boxer beating the air. No, I strike a blow to my body and make it my slave so that after I have preached to others, I myself will not be disqualified for the prize.

The Apostle Paul makes it clear that the point is not whether we come in first place, but that we stick with the training, discipline, and run to finish, that we may receive the crown of life to win forever.

How do ministers run this race if they have no idea of the realities of ministry? Here are ten realities of ministry, keys for preparedness and expectation, that can help you run that race, if you are truly called to ministry.

Ministry does not get easier with time

When people speak about ministry getting easier with time, they're referring to the fact that seasoned ministers often handle things better than newer ministers. But this doesn't mean ministry gets easier with time. Saying such causes true confusion and deception about ministry work. Ministry is not a work that ever becomes easier. While it is true that we may move out of older difficulties, we are only moving into newer ones. The bigger a ministry gets, the more responsibility comes with it. The more opportunities for ministry appear, the more choices and decisions must be made. The more money a ministry acquires, the more business sense a leader must have. Ministry is still a business, albeit it is Kingdom business. Just as with any business, increase demands more attention to detail and precision.

Ministry calling and spiritual life do not ever get easier, either. Ministers must constantly face spiritual battle, issues with people who do not understand, harassment, worries, and fears, all that must be confronted and addressed with perspective, prayer, proper care, and a dedication to spiritual purpose.

Just because a larger ministry seems to have it all does not mean that it does not come at a price.

Some people you find insightful and relevant right now won't seem that way in a few years from now

As we grow in God, everyone we know doesn't always grow with us. What may seem great, fantastic, even anointed today may not seem that way in the future because our perspective changes with our level of revelation. I once knew a woman for several years who, at first, intrigued me. She seemed so disciplined and structured, and seemed so successful at what she did. I figured her to be anointed because people seemed to respond to her in a way they did not respond to me. I was so taken with her! Then the subsequent years came. She told me what to do, ordered me around, criticized me, and put me down. In her eyes, I didn't measure up. When I went in person to visit her church, my opinion of her radically changed. She had a congregation that consisted mostly of relatives and very little outside help.

Some of what seemed deep now seems...different. There are many, many other circumstances I could also draw upon that are similar inasmuch as that the people don't seem the same several years into the future. I know ministers who used to love big name preachers only to withdraw from interest, because they outgrow their teachings. If we knew now what we will know then, our perspectives on some of the people we follow – and those in our lives – would be radically different.

Not having enough money is not your problem

In our modern world, we attach great value to the idea of money. A lack of money is our excuse for not paying bills on time, for not attending events or giving to others, and yes, for obeying God. Before anyone objects, yes, it takes money to do ministry. We don't live in a world where divine providence flies down on angel wings. All throughout Scripture, God's ministry provision came through the people who were part of the work. This means the solutions to lack of money are solved with community giving, financial responsibility, and financial accountability.

This being said: you may very well not have the money you need for the work you want to do (or the bigger picture God calls you to do). It's also not going to come if you wait to start ministry because you don't have the money. God knows what we have when we start, and He can also do a lot with a little. Be creative and clever with what you have! Find ways to make the money go far and work with what you have instead of trying to get more. If you can't handle and work with the little amount you have, what makes you think God should give you more?

God gives homework – and you're not going to always like the assignments!

When I speak of God giving homework, I don't mean our spiritual lives are a gigantic test. Our lives tend to move cyclically, with various lessons and experiences repeated throughout the years. That being said, God does give us assignments, things to work on and complete in our own time. And much of what He gives, we won't like.

Serving others. Dealing with personal selfishness and shortcomings. Overcoming hurt. Examining areas for growth and greater faith. Trusting God, even when it's hard or it hurts. Ministry is a stewardship, something God entrusts us to do – and that means we must trust Him as He takes us through the more difficult aspects of our spiritual growth.

Ministry is more than entertaining sermons and fancy titles

I've met many who treat the titles of "apostle" or "prophet" as if they are nothing more than empty words. They have no connection to lead others and do nothing but scream and cry for two hours. It's grown to bother me. When I see this, it's no wonder to me that church is totally confused about the Ephesians 4:11 ministry and what each office does! Screaming, crying, and being entertaining are not in the list of apostle's duties (or any other office of the Ephesians 4:11 ministry). The word "apostle" doesn't mean "motivational speaker." Anyone can get up in a pulpit and scream and cry, running around using a ministry calling as a title. Not everyone can truly walk the day-in and day-out requirements of being an apostle, prophet, evangelist, pastor, or teacher. Ministry is not made in the pulpit. It is made in the everyday lives, conducts, encounters, and commitments we make to follow through on our missions from God. Can't return a phone call, you prompted someone to make? Can't answer questions for an interview? Can't get back to someone with an article or other item by a deadline? Don't claim to be an apostle (or anything else for that matter).

Ministers must know the Word, not just quote from the Bible

The Bible is the Scriptures. We often call the Bible "the Word," and in some semblance, this isn't incorrect. The Scriptures are the inspired word of God, thus we call it "the Word." However, the Bible teaches us that the Word is Jesus Christ. If we want to understand God's Word, we must know the Word, Jesus Christ. We can quote from the Bible as much as we like, but if we do not know the Word, we won't be able to educate others in God's Word.

For years, a very well-known minister got on television every week and read a long list of Bible verses from a teleprompter that (supposedly) proved his points about current news headlines. His style might have been famous, but it didn't prove he knew what the Bible was about. Any one of us can look up a subject in a concordance and quote a long list of Bible verses on that subject. Truly understanding God's written Word – beyond words on a page into an area of depth, history, practicality, and understandability comes first from knowing the Word, Jesus. We need to not just prattle off a verse for everything, we must truly know the Bible. This also means we must know the Bible beyond personal or private revelation into a realm that is understandable, teachable, and embraceable by many, rather than just a few.

You will face opposition

When I was around 11 years old, I was playing with Barbie dolls with my friend from down the street. She decided she was going to do some decorating on my dollhouse – without my permission. She took whatever she wanted to put on the dollhouse and proceeded to do so, and I wasn't going to have it. We had a big fight. When I told her no, she said yes, made me the whole problem, and stormed out of my playroom and went home. We didn't talk for several weeks.

Even though we are (supposedly) all grown up and more mature, we're going to have an awful lot of people who want to decorate our ministries in one way or another….and we simply can't have it. People who contact us to argue about doctrine (the issue of women in ministry, spiritual gifts, denominational struggles, etc.) really don't want to talk or expand themselves, but want to change our minds, perceiving we have stepped out of a controllable area. The same is true with areas of critique, protesters, those who become difficult or out of line, and those who use the public arena to draw attention to their own beliefs are striving for control, opposing the work of the Kingdom to bring the focus to themselves and what they do.

Not everyone is going to like what we do, not everyone is going to like us. It can't crush us. We must have a thicker hide, not falling into pieces every time someone calls us a bad word or tells us off spiritually. If setting the boundary means someone storms (metaphorically) home and doesn't talk to us for awhile (or again), then that's the way it's going to be.

Ministry choices are not easy

I think we expect the ministry experience to be easier than it really is. We think God is going to send an angel on our shoulder to make all our decisions and speak Bible verses in our ears, so we know what to do in any given situation. The choices we face in ministry are not always easy. Despite conventional notions, we can't have it all, and some of the decisions we make in the pursuit of personal lives, ministry careers, and deeper anointing all at once will mean someone or something along the way gets hurt, offended, cut out of the picture, or has to wait for later. When it comes to decisions about ministry direction, advice can be great, but the ultimate one who must be accountable for the decision is you, the minister. Challenges, quandaries, and difficult circumstances must be accepted as a part of ministry life if you are to make it as a minister.

We will tell the story how we've overcome...and we will understand it better by and by

The words to the chorus of the song, *We'll Understand it Better by and by*, are as follows:

By and by, when the morning comes,
When the saints of God are gathered home.
We will tell the story how we've overcome
We will understand it better by and by.

While the song is undeniably about life after the Second Coming of Christ, there is something true about its lyrics for life this side of heaven, as well. In ministry, we don't understand a lot of what we go through when we go through it. We don't understand why God has us do certain things, walk through certain trials, or have certain experiences. Many never understand what they go through because they never get beyond their experiences but simply keep repeating mistakes and choices that cause them to go through the same problems over and over again. As overcomers, God calls His ministers to reach the point of "by and by," where they can stand back, having overcome their difficulties and trials. Even though it seems hard to get through, we have to reach the point of "by and by" to have our circumstances make sense. In the world, they say hindsight is 20/20. Our spiritual hindsight is in the "by and by."

Ministry life won't always be what you hoped it to become

Once upon a time, an old friend of mine (who was also an apostle) told me of a woman under her ministry who believed she too was called to be an apostle. She had it all planned out: she was going to have a nanny and travel with a professional hairdresser. To this woman, this was what being an apostle is about – even though she watched both my friend and me for years in ministry. While both my friend and I knew this woman will never have what she wanted, her aspirations used to give us a good laugh when we were having a bad day. Her aspirations also reveal a common problem about ministry: we overestimate ministry life. People who aren't in ministry think ministers walk around on a cloud, wearing white, singing the Hallelujah Chorus all day. Many think ministers have no problems, challenges, or difficulties because "God takes care of them." These delusions of ministry life have flooded over to ministers themselves, who enter ministry with warped concepts about bills, money, payments, preaching engagements, travel, ministry response, and the like. Just like everyone else, every minister has their days when they wonder what their life would have been like had they done something else with it and fight discouragement, despair, depression, and stress. Not every minister likes every aspect of what they do in ministry; in fact, I would venture most ministers dislike something about what they are called to do. While it may not be the calling itself, there are plenty of things tagged on to having a calling that can prove difficult or unpleasant. Anyone who indicates anything else is lying or not in ministry deep enough to experience the true sacrifice every minister must experience.

CHAPTER FIFTEEN

★ ★ ★

DISCUSSION POINTS: KEYS FOR FURTHER HELPS MINISTRIES TRAINING

Nevertheless, the one who receives instruction in the word should share all good things with their instructor.
(Galatians 6:6)

THIS chapter is a final look at helps ministries with one of the most important aspects of helps ministry: good communication between a leader and a helps minister. In these final pages, we are going to look at some talking points to start dialogue between a leader and a helps minister in training. This chapter is also a launching point for the specifics of helps ministry training that we are unable to cover in this book, because they are unique to your specific ministry.

Every leader has specific ways they may want something done. Throughout this book, you have found some basic guidelines to help start a work in helps ministry. The specifics of how to do helps ministry, however, often come from a leader and come forth in the training process. This book is just the beginning of the specific and wonderful thoughts that will come forth from your helps ministry experience.

Questions to ask your leader

- What are the specifics of the ministry I will be working in?
- Who else will I be working with?
- Who will I directly answer to in this helps ministry work?
- How often will I be called upon for service?
- What attire is required?
- What is expected of me in this helps ministry service?

- How often will there be regularly scheduled helps ministry meetings?
- Will there be any written or study assignments in keeping with my work in helps ministry?

Talking points/questions your leader should discuss/ask you

- Explain the importance of helps ministries to the church or ministry that you are a part of.
- Why is being a part of helps ministry important to you?
- What is special about the helps ministry you will be participating in?
- Do you understand the responsibilities and duties that go along with your helps ministry assignment?

Writing assignments for the helps minister

- What is your concept of helps ministries and what they do?
- Why do you believe helps ministries are important?
- Why do you believe you desire to work in your specific area of helps ministries?
- In looking at the appointments and works of the church in the Word, why do you believe God established the entire ministry of helps?
- What are some wrong reasons to desire helps ministry? What are some right reasons?
- List some of the duties and responsibilities you have as a helps minister.

Scriptures for study for helps ministers

- Matthew 25:31-46
- Matthew 10:41
- Luke 19:11-27
- Luke 22:26
- Acts 6:1-15
- Acts 20:17-31
- Acts 28:10

- Romans 12:4-6
- Romans 16:1-23
- 1 Corinthians 9:24-27
- 1 Corinthians 12:5
- 1 Corinthians 16:12-20
- 2 Corinthians 9:12
- Galatians 6:6
- Ephesians 2:20
- Ephesians 4:1
- Ephesians 4:11-16
- Ephesians 6:21-22
- Colossians 4:7-17
- 1 Timothy 3:1-13
- 1 Timothy 5:17-18
- Titus 1:6-16
- Titus 2:1-5
- Hebrews 13:7
- Hebrews 13:17
- James 5:14-15
- 1 Peter 5:1-10
- 2 Peter 1:10
- 2 Peter 2:19-25
- Revelation 5:5-14

ASSIGNMENTS

——— ★ ★ ★ ———

Short answer
(Using the text, answer the following questions in approximately one to four sentences each.)

1. Why is it important for a minister to recognize the relevance of service and helps ministries?

2. Why is ministry training important?

3. How should we handle ourselves when experiencing different types of worship services that vary from our own?

4. What is a minister's license? What is ordination? How do the two vary? How does a legitimate minister's license vary from one you can randomly obtain online?

Essay
(Answer the questions in essay format. Spelling and grammar count. Each essay must be at least 3-5 sentences in length [longer essays are permitted].)

1. Explain the different spiritual gifts. Why are these gifts important? How do these gifts vary from an anointing?

2. Describe the appointment works and how they differ from Ephesians 4:11 ministry leadership. What are the appointments? Why are the appointments important? How are they misunderstood? What are some examples of ministry that the different appointment offices would oversee?

3. What are some of the criteria for a helps minister? Why do helps ministers have such extensive criteria and requirements? Why are these requirements so important?

4. What does it mean to have a "covering" and why is this relationship important in the life of ministry? How do you interact with your leader, and your leader with you?

Projects

(Complete the projects according to the directions and the direction of your instructor.)

1. Implement a church "helps ministries" program package. Write out the different programs needed in a church, which appointments or ministers will oversee them, and how they will function.

2. List the different types of attire.

3. List different pieces of ceremonial attire.

4. List garments every minister should have.

Final exam

Answer questions and complete writing assignments as found in Chapter 15. From the Scripture list that is available, use several of them in your answers. If your leader is available, this can be done in a discussion format.

ABOUT THE AUTHOR

★ ★ ★

DR. LEE ANN B. MARINO, PH.D., D.MIN., D.D. (she/her) is "everyone's favorite theologian" leading Gen X, Millennials, and Gen Z with expertise in leadership training, queer and feminist theology, general religion, and apostolic theology. She has served in ministry since 1998 and was ordained as a pastor in 2002 and an apostle in 2010. She founded what is now Sanctuary Apostolic Fellowship Empowerment (SAFE) Ministries in 2004. Under her ministry heading Dr. Marino is founder and Overseer of Sanctuary International Fellowship Tabernacle (SIFT) (the original home of National Coming Out Sunday) and The Sanctuary Network, and Chancellor of Apostolic Covenant Theological Seminary (ACTS).

Affectionately nicknamed "the Spitfire," Dr. Marino has spent over two decades as an "apostle, preacher, and teacher" (2 Timothy 1:11), exercising her personal mandate to become "all things to all people" (1 Corinthians 9:22). Her embrace of spiritual issues (both technical and intimate) has found its home among both seekers and believers, those who desire spiritual answers to today's issues.

Dr. Marino has preached throughout the United States, Puerto Rico, and Europe in hundreds of religious services and experiences throughout the years. A history maker in her own right, she has spent over two decades in advocacy, education, and work for and within minority spiritual communities (including African American, Hispanic, and LGBTQ+). She has also served as the first woman on all-male synods, councils, and panels, as well as the first preacher or speaker welcomed of a different race, sexual orientation, or identity among diverse communities. Today, Dr. Marino's work extends to over 150 countries as she hosts the popular *Kingdom Now* podcast, which is in the top 20 percentile of all podcasts worldwide. She is also the author of over 35 books and the popular Patheos column, *Leadership on Fire*. To date, she has had five bestselling titles within their subject matter: *Understanding Demonology, Spiritual Warfare, Healing, and Deliverance: A Manual for the Christian Minister; Ministry School Boot Camp: Training for Helps Ministries, Appointments, and Beyond; Discovering Intimacy: A Journey Through the Song of Solomon; Fruit of the Vine: Study and Commentary on the Fruit of the Spirit;* and *Ministering to LGBTQ+ (and Those Who Love Them): A Primer for Queer Theology* (and its accompanying workbook).

As a public icon and social media influencer, Dr. Marino advocates healthy body image (curvy/full-figured), representation as a demisexual/aromantic, and albinism awareness as a model. Known to those she works with, she is a spiritual mom, teacher, leader, professor, confidant, and friend. She continues to transform, receiving new teaching, revelation, and insight in this thing we call "ministry." Through years of spiritual growth and maturity, Dr. Marino stands as herself, here to present what God has given to her for any who have an ear to hear.

For more information, visit her website at kingdompowernow.org.

www.ingramcontent.com/pod-product-compliance
Lightning Source LLC
LaVergne TN
LVHW011201080426
835508LV00007B/531